MARINE WILDLIFE

of Puget Sound, the San Juans,
and the Strait of Georgia

D0190474

MARINE WILDLIFE

of Puget Sound, the San Juans, and
the Strait of Georgia

by Steve Yates

The Globe Pequot Press

Chester, Connecticut 06412

To David B. and Kathryn Yates,
for their encouragement and support.

Copyright 1988 by Steve Yates
Marine mammal and bird illustrations copyright 1988 by Fred Sharpe
Invertebrate and botanical illustrations copyright 1988 by Catherine
    Eaton Skinner

Permission to use fish illustrations by D. R. Harriott from *Pacific
Fishes of Canada* by J. L. Hart (published by the Fisheries Research
Board of Canada) granted by Pacific Fisheries of Canada, Department
of Fisheries and Oceans.

MANUFACTURED IN THE UNITED STATES OF AMERICA
FIRST EDITION
FIRST PRINTING

Library of Congress Cataloging-in-Publication Data

Yates, Steven A.
    Marine wildlife of Puget Sound, the San Juans, and Strait of
Georgia / by Steve Yates ; illustrations by Catherine Eaton Skinner,
Fred Sharpe, and D.R. Harriott. -- 1st ed.
    p. cm.
  Bibliography: p.
  Includes index.
  ISBN 0-87106-660-2
  1. Marine fauna--Washington (State)--Identification.   2. Marine
fauna--British Columbia--Identification.   3. Sea birds--Washington
(State)--Identification.   4. Sea birds--British Columbia-
-Identification.   5. Marine algae--Washington (State)-
-Identification.   6. Marine algae--British Columbia--Identification.
I. Title.
QL212.Y38 1988
574.92'632--dc 19   88-2356
                                                          CIP

Book and cover designs by Judy Petry

Contents

Acknowledgments

Although I have spent time observing most of the marine mammals, birds, fishes, invertebrates, and seaweeds described in this guide, I am no expert in any of these fields. This book owes a great debt to those countless biologists who have, for their own reasons, painstakingly studied, sampled, measured, weighed, pumped stomachs, sorted prey items, and observed ranges for the more than three hundred species described in this guide.

I am especially grateful to those naturalists who have put their own and others' findings into books and keys, some of which have guided my own education in the field; they have also contributed numerous facts and observations to this guide. Foremost among these are Dr. Eugene Kozloff's *Seashore Life of the Northern Pacific Coast* and his key to the *Marine Invertebrates of the Pacific Northwest;* Tony Angell and Ken Balcomb's *Marine Birds and Mammals of Puget Sound;* and *Marine Mammals of Greater Puget Sound: A Naturalist's Field Guide,* by Rich Osborne, John Calambokidis, and Ellie Dorsey. I am also indebted to all the authors and illustrators of the many other excellent guides listed in the bibliography.

I also wish to thank those who offered to read and comment on the manuscript, especially Mark Lewis (birds); Dr. Charles 'Si' Simenstad (fishes); Richard Osborne (marine mammals); Charles Eaton (invertebrates); and Dr. Ron Thom (seaweeds). Without them there would be more errors and fewer interesting facts.

Illustrators Catherine Eaton Skinner (invertebrates and seaweeds) and Fred Sharpe (marine mammals and birds) are keen naturalists and excellent artists; I am proud to have worked with them.

D. R. Harriott's fish illustrations were originally done under the supervision of Dr. J. L. Hart for his classic *Pacific Fishes of Canada.* I am grateful for Mr. Harriott's kind cooperation and for the assistance of John Camp of the Information and Publications Branch, Department of Fisheries and Oceans Canada, and Bonnie Livingston of the National Museum of Canada for locating and sending the original photostats stored at the museum. Permission to reprint was given by the Department of Fisheries and Oceans Canada.

Finally, I would like to thank Carolyn Threadgill, West Coast consultant for Globe Pequot Press, who enthusiastically endorsed this project from the beginning; editor Margaret Foster-Finan; book designer Judy Petry; and Globe Pequot's Director of Publications, Linda Kennedy, and her able staff.

Thanks also to my birding and tide-pooling partner, Lea Mitchell, for many enjoyable trips to the field.

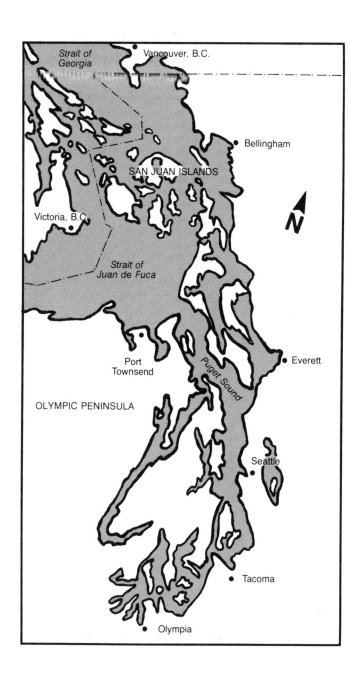

Strait of
Georgia

Vancouver, B.C.

Bellingham

SAN JUAN ISLANDS

Victoria, B.C.

Strait of
Juan de Fuca

N

Port
Townsend

Everett

OLYMPIC PENINSULA

Puget Sound

Seattle

Tacoma

Olympia

Introduction

Off the shore of Seattle's Discovery Park a flock of common terns —graceful "sea-swallows" with slender wings and long, forked tails —spot dinner below. One, then another plunges headfirst from thirty feet. As one tern rises, a sand lance wriggling from its forecepslike bill, a larger bird approaches from above. Its head is gullish, its body robust; but the sharp wings are falconlike, and a pair of pointed feathers extends from its wedge-shaped tail. Spotting the successful tern, the parasitic jaeger swoops.

The tern avoids the dive adroitly and darts away. It gains altitude, but the jaeger is soon on it. The tern zigs and zags; dives, twists, and rises. The pirate shadows it move for move. The tern's acrobatic flight is impressive, but the larger bird's maneuvers are stunning. Defeated, the tern drops the silvery fish. The jaeger snatches it deftly from midair.

In the Strait of Juan de Fuca, south of San Juan Island, an excited flock of gulls, murres, and auklets scatters from the boiling surface as a solitary Minke whale lunges up to engulf an entire school of herring. To the north, up Haro Strait, a pod of Dall's porpoises feeds leisurely on darting squid—submerging with a motion that inspired Indians to call them "broken-backs." As a powerboat passes nearby, the sleek porpoises pursue it, kicking up rooster tails of spray. Puffing explosively at the surface, they surf the boat's bow wave, almost close enough to touch.

At the southern end of Hood Canal, two-foot-long chum salmon in ragged breeding colors fight their way up a shallow creek tumbling through Twanoh State Park. Off the stream's mouth, dogfish sharks feed on salmon carcasses; flocks of gulls and crows pick at the dying fish stranded along the creek's sides. Only a few of the salmon manage to struggle through the chutes from pool to pool to finally gain the riffles above. There, in the foggy cedar woods, they spend their last gasp of energy to lay and fertilize the precious eggs that justify the long, dangerous journey home.

These are just a few of the more spectacular large-scale scenes from the continuous, free pageant put on by the marine wildlife of our inland waters. Just as engrossing are the smaller-scale dramas that can be seen close up every time we peer into a rocky tide pool full of hermit crabs and tidepool sculpins, or watch a great blue heron stalking fish on the shoreline. Low tide uncovers some four thousand miles of rocky shore, cobble and sand beaches, tideflats, and salt marshes to the curious beachcomber. Each tide zone and each habitat type hosts a different mix of animals and seaweeds; the extreme low tides of spring and summer expose many others to view.

Below the tides, scuba divers explore rock gardens, kelp forests, and seagrass meadows that rival the tropics in color and diversity. Beneath the surface of our fertile fjords, rock walls teem with colorful feather duster worms, giant sunflower stars, and iridescent seaweeds. Schools of shiner perch and striped seaperch drift between old piers transformed into fantasy gardens by thick growths of tall, white plumed anemones. Cabezons and red Irish lords lurk on the bottom among darting coon-stripe shrimp and boldly striped painted greenlings. More than two hundred species of marine fishes have been recorded from local waters—three times the number found in San Francisco Bay. Eight species of anadromous salmon and trout —as fascinating to observe in the wild as they are delicious on the table—spend all or part of their marine lives in the inland sea before returning to the basin's streams to spawn.

Sheltered from the frequent storms and pounding surf of the outer coast, the island-studded inland waters give winter refuge to dozens of species of seabirds, shorebirds, and waterfowl; many others, like the terns and jaeger, pass through the area during spring and fall migrations. Tufted puffins, rhinoceros auklets, and other seabirds arrive by the thousands each summer to breed on protected islands and islets. Bald eagles, great blue herons, and belted kingfishers can be found along the shores year-round.

California and northern sea lions winter here in increasing numbers. Dall's porpoises, harbor porpoises, and Minke whales ply the passages around the San Juan and Canadian Gulf islands, their numbers swelling in summer. Curious harbor seals and slithery river otters can be enjoyed in all seasons. Orca whales still breech and spy hop against glacial cliffs and city skylines—a front yard extravaganza that shames any marine amusement park.

That such a wildlife paradise still coexists with a surrounding human population of nearly four million is nothing short of amazing. But though we can enjoy our good fortune, we cannot take it for granted. Wild salmon stocks have been decimated by overharvesting and loss of spawning streams. Waterfowl numbers declined precipitously as estuaries were dredged and filled for industrial waterways and river deltas diked for farmland. Increasingly toxic pollutants now threaten the aquatic habitat on which local marine communities (human and wildlife) depend. Toxic sediments have poisoned gray whales and caused cancerous lesions in bottom fishes. Shellfish beds accumulate coliform bacteria from storm runoff, leaky septic systems, and municipal sewage. Seabirds remain vulnerable to oil spills as tankers ply our narrow, rocky channels.

The more we learn about the fascinating lives of marine wildlife, the more we understand the impact that we—as individuals and as a society—have on the beautiful aquatic creatures living in our bays and estuaries. Only an informed, active appreciation will enable us to preserve this rich natural heritage.

■ THIS BOOK

Whether you are a birder or tide pooler; a boater, kayaker, fisherman, or ferry rider; a shoreline homeowner; a young naturalist or parent of curious youngsters; a visitor to our fine saltwater parks, a vacationer, or just a casual beachcomber, this portable guidebook, carried in a daypack or jacket pocket, will add further dimensions to your travels on and around the inland waters.

It introduces the cast of colorful characters that add drama to our beachcombing, boating, or diving experiences and also gives some background on the players' roles and interactions. By noting who does what and who eats whom, it will become clear that the species included in this book are inextricably intertwined. By also noting our own diet and activities, it should be equally clear that our lives and theirs are similarly intertwined.

Until now, information about local marine animals and seaweeds has been scattered among many separate books. Most treat just a single group of animals over a much wider geographic area; others are written for the advanced naturalist. And some so-called field guides, though useful as references, are not rugged enough to survive many trips to the field. This durable five-in-one guide includes all the local marine mammals, seabirds, fishes, invertebrates, and seaweeds most apt to be encountered during a beach walk or scuba dive, or seen from a kayak, fishing boat, or ferry.

■ AREA COVERED

This guide was designed to be used on and around the inland waters of Washington and southern British Columbia. Its western boundary is somewhat arbitrary, but a line from Dungeness Spit on the Olympic Peninsula north to Victoria or Race Rocks on southeastern Vancouver Island would be a good approximation. Though most of the species included here will be seen westward of that line, many of the shorebirds, waterfowl, and estuarine invertebrates are limited to the more sheltered inland channels. The lack of sheltered bays along the western end of the Strait of Juan de Fuca, and the heavy swells that roll unhindered from the Pacific give those waters a decidedly oceanic character; and species such as the goose barnacle and sea palm, northern fulmar and storm-petrel, pilot whale and white-sided dolphin are largely restricted to the western end of the strait. Some of these oceanic species may also be found around the more exposed shores of southern San Juan and Lopez islands and the west side of northern Whidbey Island, but in order to keep this guide compact, they will not be given full descriptions.

■ IDENTIFICATION HINTS

First observe the general shape of the animal or seaweed. Note special features such as the bill or head shape of a bird, the dorsal fin of a whale, the outline of a fish, or the size and shape of a kelp. The dividers that separate the five sections will indicate the pages on which that general group of organisms will be found.

Check for unique features or color patterns in the text opposite the possible candidates. Also check preferred habitat—some creatures are restricted to rocky shores or mud flats, to high tide levels, or to the subtidal zone. Watch also for distinctive patterns of behavior, such as the way a seabird dives or flies; these will often allow you to identify the species even when you are too far away to see details of form or color.

As noted in the text, colors of fishes and invertebrates can vary significantly. Bird plumage patterns are reliable in midwinter and in summer, but can be more difficult to decipher in spring and fall as the birds gain or lose breeding plumage. Fortunately, birds usually are seen in pairs or flocks, and a nearby individual may be more clearly marked.

Sizes given for birds are from life, not stretched museum skins. Many fishes, invertebrates, and algae continue to grow throughout their lifetimes, though growth slows with age. Sizes given for these groups are the approximate maximums for the species. Most local individuals will be smaller, but larger ones sometimes will be seen.

Field identification can be frustrating when an individual creature refuses to conform to the generalization of a field guide, especially one like this, which strives to be compact rather than exhaustive. Like humans, most species contain many races and a variety of individual differences, both in color pattern and behavior. But patience (and a good pair of binoculars) will usually unravel the most difficult cases. Getting to know a new species can be as satisfying as meeting a new friend.

■HABITATS

This guide is not divided by habitat—rocky shore, sandy beach, salt marsh, and muddy bay—though preferred habitat for each species is noted in the text. For benthic (attached) or burrowing creatures, substrate (bottom material) is a major component of habitat. Animals such as barnacles, mussels, and limpets obviously need a rock or wood surface to attach to, and most clams and worms can only burrow into mud or sand. But many of the mobile animals are found on or over a variety of substrates. And though many species are dependent on a single substrate for shelter or prey, the intermix of substrates in the inland waters makes it impractical to make too fine a point of this.

Some animals and seaweeds require strong waves and currents, while others thrive only in quiet backwaters. Exposure to waves and current may differ from shore to nearby shore, even within a single bay, depending on orientation and on the protective influences of headlands, reefs, and islands. Storm waves and currents also indirectly influence biocommunities by changing the substrate as they erode and deposit gravels, sand, and silt.

The surface of inner Puget Sound is covered by hundreds of feet of glacial till—a mix of cobble and sand—often underlain by thick layers of clay. Where currents are strong enough to carry away the smaller material, the beaches below the eroding glacial cliffs are cobbly; where currents are weak, sand or silt may cover the larger material. In general the southern beaches can only be classified as "mixed."

To the north, the shores of the San Juan and Canadian Gulf islands are mostly rocky; though here, too, we find large areas of glacial deposition. Local rivers carry heavy loads of sediments, and so the shores around river mouths are generally silty. Inlets and bays, where currents are weak, also collect fine sediments.

Glacial processes and tidal currents, along with significant human intervention, have all caused sediments to be distributed in unexpected ways. Sandy or shelly "pocket beaches" interrupt rocky shores; glacial erratics, drift logs, and wooden pilings are found on otherwise soft beaches; and former salt marshes have been diked or filled, converting them to freshwater marshes or farmland. Some substrates are stable, others unstable—sand beaches can be built up in summer and removed by winter storms.

In geologic terms, the entire area is unstable. An enormous ice sheet scraped out these fjords only twelve millennia ago. Inner Puget Sound was a freshwater lake for centuries; water levels have changed radically, and eroded glacial drift has been filling up the edges ever since the mile-thick tongue of ice withdrew.

■ TIDES

As extensions of the Pacific Ocean, the deep fjords and shallow inlets that make up our inland waterways are strongly affected by tides and tidal currents. Fish move in over beaches with the incoming tide, and they congregate where converging currents concentrate prey organisms. Seabirds, marine mammals, and human anglers follow the movements of the fishes. When the tide is out, intertidal animals are exposed to the air, to the drying rays of the sun, and to extreme changes in temperature and salinity. Shorebirds, wading birds, and scavengers feed at low tide; during daylight lows, human tide poolers and clam diggers also converge on the shore. Prudent kayakers and scuba divers wait for slack tides to avoid potentially dangerous tidal currents.

The heights and timing of the tides depend on a number of factors. Most important are the changing but predictable positions of moon and sun relative to the earth. Much less predictable, but also much less important, are the effects of winds, barometric pressure, and river runoff.

Though the moon is much smaller than the sun, it is also much closer to the earth and therefore exerts more gravitational pull on the earth's surface. This attraction has only a minute effect on the solid crust of the continents, but a considerable effect on the liquid surface of the sea, causing it to bulge in the area closest to the moon (a similar bulge forms on the side farthest from it). As the earth rotates westward during the day, the bulges (and the depressions between) appear to move eastward like a long wave with a period of just over twelve hours between peaks. We experience the wave as a twice-a-day set of rising and falling tides.

Ideally, the tide would rise and fall at the same time at any meridian of longitude. But motion caused by the rough terrain and by offshore islands and channels slows and distorts the wave. High tide occurs an hour later at Olympia, for example, than at Port Townsend even though both are on about the same meridian.

Near full or new moons (when the moon and sun are in line with the earth) the combined forces of moon and sun exaggerate the tidal bulges. We call these "spring" tides (after the Saxon word *springan,* to jump or rise). As the moon moves to a ninety-degree angle to the sun (relative to earth), the two gravitational forces partially cancel each other out, smoothing out the bulge into gentler "neap" tides (after the Saxon *neafte,* scarce). And so the tidal range (difference between high and low tides) varies throughout the month, from about ten to fifteen feet (depending on location) near full moon to only five to eight feet near half moon. The tidal range also varies during the year as earth, moon, and sun move closer or farther apart during their eliptical orbits.

Our local tides are called "mixed diurnal" because the two daily highs are unequal, and the lows even more so. In the inland waters, a very low tide is usually followed by a very high tide, and then a medium low tide by a medium high tide. The graph below represents a week of spring tides in Puget Sound.

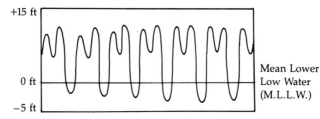

+15 ft

0 ft — Mean Lower Low Water (M.L.L.W.)

−5 ft

As the tide wave is squeezed through the straits and inter-island channels, it creates strong tidal currents (as anyone who has kayaked or dived in the San Juan or Canadian Gulf islands or has run The Narrows or Deception Pass in a small craft well knows). The boiling tidal rips are a principal reason why our inland waters are so rich in marine wildlife. Currents and upwellings mix the waters, bringing nutrients to upper layers that would otherwise be depleted; and they suspend plankton and detritus that would otherwise settle to the bottom. This mixing allows the single-celled plants—diatoms and dinoflagellates—to bloom (multiply greatly) whenever there is enough sunshine, plus proper temperature and salinity. Zooplankton—tiny crustaceans and the larvae of larger animals—then feed on the phytoplankton. This rich, organic soup supports large populations of crustaceans, small fishes, and squids on which our larger fishes, seabirds, and marine mammals feast.

The timing of seasonal spring tides is also important. Locally, in winter extreme low tides occur at night, exposing intertidal animals to freezing temperatures. In summer the lowest tides occur at mid-day, exposing them to the full power of the drying sun, and also to the greatest concentration of beach-loving humans and dogs. These stresses greatly influence the makeup of the intertidal community, making it critical that we be sensitive while exploring the seashore.

■ SEASHORE MANNERS

As the number of homeowners, beachcombers, clammers, dog walkers, fishermen, kayakers, and scuba divers grows, so does our impact on marine wildlife. The following guidelines will help lessen this impact.

- After inspecting an intertidal rock, turn it back to its original orientation. Creatures living under rocks need protection or shade; creatures that live on top of rocks need light or food-rich currents. Both kinds may die when rocks are left overturned. Replace the rock gently, so as not to crush the animals beneath.
- The cover formed by seaweeds at low tides keeps intertidal crea-tures from drying out and hides them from predators. Replace this cover after looking under it for interesting organisms.
- Do not collect animals where prohibited. Without sanctuaries, pop-ulations will dwindle and scientists, naturalists, and school-children will be deprived of study sites. Do not collect unnecessar-ily. All animals are more interesting alive than dead. Most crea-tures brought home from the shore soon lose their shape and color; most will just end up smelly in the trash instead of alive and color-ful in the sea.
- Refill holes when digging for clams. Abandoned piles of sand will suffocate small clams and other burrowing animals.
- Watch where you walk. It is easy to trample small organisms and scare off foraging birds.
- Restrain dogs on beaches. Shorebirds and beach scavengers feed only at low tides, and there is little more annoying to other nature observers than a barking dog running down a quiet beach, chasing off all the birds.
- The number of scuba divers is growing rapidly, while accessible dive sites are limited. Animals such as abalone, octopus, and ling-cod can be wiped out of heavily used areas (octopus and lingcod are especially vulnerable when guarding their eggs in the shal-lows). Respect bag limits and do not collect in marine preserves. Underwater photographers and nonconsumptive divers deserve the chance to enjoy intact marine communities.
- Harbor seals must haul out on rocks daily to gather warmth, and seasonally to give birth to their pups. Since seals are clumsy on

land, they are easily disturbed. Do not approach too closely by boat or when walking haul-out beaches.

- Small islands and islets are also crucial to seabirds as breeding or roosting sites. When parent birds are disturbed from their nests, the eggs or nestlings are vulnerable to gulls, crows, and other predators.

- Orcas (killer whales) are exciting to observe, and they do not seem to be hesitant about approaching boaters. Their harassment is strictly prohibited by the Marine Mammal Protection Act. Boats should approach no closer than one hundred yards and should run slowly, parallel to the path of the whales. Avoid fast or unpredictable movements and shut down the engine if a whale surfaces nearby. Try not to cross the whales' path or force them to change course.

- How closely an animal will allow you to approach depends upon a number of factors. A slow, quiet, relaxed (nonpredatory) approach will get you closest, especially if the animal is allowed clear avenues of escape. Animal species differ greatly in their tolerance; some species are naturally shy, while others may be playful or curious (the harbor porpoise, for example, avoids powerboats, while its close relative the Dall's porpoise will often come over to a boat to ride the bow wave). Birds that take time to get airborne (cormorants, for example) tend to be more wary than those that can rise easily (mallards and other dabbling ducks). Seals, after a commercial fishing opening, and waterfowl, during hunting seasons, will be especially nervous.

In mixed flocks, the most skitterish species may cause the whole group to flee. As soon as the nearest animals begin to get fidgety, it is time to stop and quietly observe. A pair of binoculars or a spotting scope is by far the easiest—and often the only—way to see most wild animals close up.

■NAMES

Scientists have given each plant and animal species a two-part, latinized name. The first, or generic, part is always capitalized. It refers to the genus, a group of closely related species (all local rockfishes, for example, are of the genus *Sebastes*). The second, or specific, part is never capitalized. It refers to the unique species (*Sebastes melanops*, the black rockfish). The advantage of a scientific name is that each species has only one name that is accepted worldwide (though it may change as new relationships are discovered).

Most of the more visible species also have at least one common name. A common name, though easier to remember, often varies from region to region or among user groups. The Manila clam, for example, is also called a Japanese littleneck or is simply lumped with the native littleneck clam as a "steamer." Or the same common name might be used for many species. "Blenny eel," for example, refers to a number of slender intertidal species belonging to two similar-looking but separate fish families—the gunnels and pricklebacks.

Biologists group closely related genera (plural of genus) into families, families into orders, orders into classes, and classes into phyla (plural of phylum). Mammals, birds, and fishes, for example, are classes of vertebrates (animals with backbones) that all belong to the phylum Chordata (animals with spinal chords). Marine invertebrates, on the other hand, belong to many different phyla. In this book the names of groupings larger than genus are listed, often with description, above the first species in that particular group.

The problem of common names is compounded in a book like this, which contains five categories of animals and plants. Birds have well-accepted common names that are regularly updated in the American Ornithologists' Union (A.O.U.) *Check-list of North American Birds.* Fishes also have a regulated list of common names, which is gradually gaining acceptance. For many of the smaller intertidal invertebrates and seaweeds, however, scientific names are all we have. Where an animal or plant does not have a widely accepted common name, I have used the generic name, without italics, as a common name (seaweeds such as Sargassum, Porphyra, and Alaria; invertebrates such as Obelia and Amphiporus). As a cross-reference, I have capitalized common names of species that are described elsewhere in the text (*e.g.*, "Feeds on Herring, sculpins, and Sand Lance.").

Bird names follow the 1983 A.O.U. *Check-list* (with July, 1985 Supplement). Fishes follow the American Fisheries Society's *A List of Common and Scientific Names of Fishes from the United States and Canada* (1980). Invertebrate names are based on *Marine Invertebrates of the Pacific Northwest* (E. N. Kozloff, 1987). Seaweeds names follow *A Synopsis of Benthic Marine Algae of British Columbia, Northern Washington and Southeast Alaska* (R. F. Scagel, *et al.*, 1986). Marine mammal names follow *Marine Birds and Mammals of Puget Sound* (Angell and Balcomb, 1982). Alternate common names and recently superceded scientific names are included in parentheses.

Within the sections, the order of the families generally follows taxonomic conventions. But sometimes it has been useful to group similar-looking families that are not closely related.

■EQUIPMENT

To go to the beach or on a boat trip without a pair of binoculars is to miss much of the wildlife—and most of the details of appearance and behavior that make wildlife observation such a pleasure. Binoculars also allow us to see a bird or seal or whale as if we were seven to ten times closer, without the disturbance that an actual approach would cause.

I use an 8 × 30 compact pair. They are always handy in my pocket. They do, however, have a narrow field of view, making it difficult to spot flying birds. Birders and boaters often prefer a larger pair with a greater field of vision: 7 × 35, 7 × 50, or 10 × 40 (the first number refers to the power, or magnification; the second to the diameter of the exit lens, in millimeters). The lower the power compared to the exit diameter, the easier it is to use on a swaying boat, and the more light it will collect at dawn or dusk. Good quality center-focus binoculars—avoid shoddy ones—are surprisingly inexpensive and durable; and even a small pocket monocular will add tremendously to one's outdoor pleasure.

On nature walks or boat trips (even ferry rides), I wear a fishing-type vest. It offers handy pockets for binoculars, field guide, notebook and pen, compass, sunglasses, sunblock and lip balm, collecting baggies, and even camera lenses. Since marine breezes are always cooler than a hreeze on land, and since local weather is rarely predictable, I always carry a day pack with light rain gear, hat, and gloves, as well as some food and juice (and for tide pooling, a change of socks).

When tide pooling, it is usually best to wear boots and rain pants (which will allow you to kneel or sit on wet rocks or seaweed). A pair of gardener's rubber knee pads can also come in handy on rocky shores. For looking at small intertidal organisms, a small net and white plastic tray of some sort are useful. Most tide poolers carry a pocket lens; I find that looking through my binocular lens in the reverse direction works almost as well.

The most important tools, of course, are sharp eyes and an appreciative, curious mind.

MARINE MAMMALS

■ Seals and Sea Lions

Order Pinnipedia

Pinnipeds (fin-foots) form an order of marine mammals that includes true, or earless, seals (*Family* Phocidae) and eared seals (sea lions and fur seals—*Family* Otariidae). They haul out (come ashore) to pup (give birth). Dense fur augments insulative blubber.

■ Seals

Family Phocidae

True seals lack external ears. Small foreflippers and immobilizing hind flippers make them extremely clumsy when hauled out on land for resting or pupping. Graceful swimmers, propelled by strong, flipper-like rear feet; use foreflippers as rudders. Efficient carnivores; feed on a variety of fishes.

■ HARBOR SEAL

Phoca vitulina

Grayish, spotted pelt. Doglike head and face. Large brown eyes. Sexes similar in size and appearance. Length to 6 feet.

Common year-round resident. Shy but curious. Seen singly or in small groups. Often floats in vertical position with head above water; sinks below surface when alarmed. On land basks near water's edge, quickly slithering into water on belly when alarmed.

Can dive to 300 feet and submerge for 20 minutes; usually just 3 to 5 minutes before bobbing up to breathe. Feeds on flounders, Herring, Walleye Pollock, cod, sculpins, Shiner Perch, and rockfishes. Also catches squids in winter and octopuses in summer. Sometimes steals netted salmon or damages nets. Fishermen and bounty hunters killed 17,000 harbor seals in Washington State between 1947 and 1960.

Since gaining protection under the National Marine Mammal Protection Act of 1972, harbor seal populations have risen rapidly. About five thousand breed locally on protected islands. Female gives birth to single pup on remote beach or log boom July through September; adults mate during that time. Live to 30 years or more.

■ NORTHERN ELEPHANT SEAL

Mirounga angustirostris

Large body; long, thick snout. Lethargic. Relatively small foreflippers. Gray-brown coloration. Largest pinniped. Male up to 3 times as heavy as female; up to 3 times as long and 20 times as heavy as male Harbor Seal. Solitary male ranges much farther north than female; seen spring and fall during migrations between northern feeding grounds from Washington to Alaska and breeding islands off California and Mexico. There, male's snout lengthens; he uses bulk to aggressively fight for beach territories and harems of females. Male: 15 to 20 feet, 2.5 to 4 tons. Female: 11 to 12 feet, 1 ton.

Feeds on bottom fishes, Spotted Ratfish, Dogfish, skates, and squids. Commonly submerges for 20 minutes; may be capable of diving to 2,500 feet. Nearly exterminated by sealers during the past century (blubber rendered for oil). Since protection under the Marine Mammal Protection Act, populations have recovered to about 100,000.

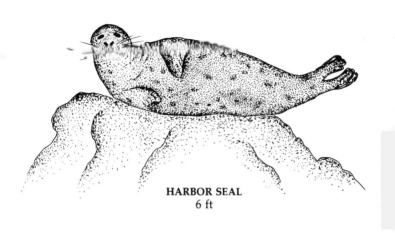

HARBOR SEAL
6 ft

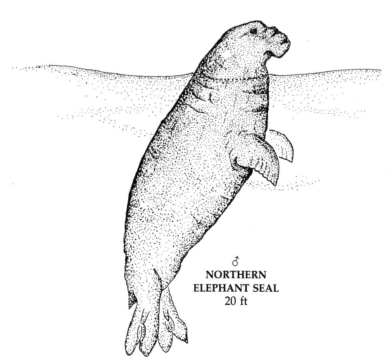

♂
**NORTHERN
ELEPHANT SEAL**
20 ft

■ Sea Lions
Family Otariidae

External ears are small but visible. Dense underfur. Hind flippers rotate, and so sea lions can hump along rapidly on land. In water propel themselves with long, paddlelike foreflippers; steer with hind flippers.

■ CALIFORNIA SEA LION
Zalophus californianus

Pelt dark brown when wet, tawny when dry. Doglike face with pointed muzzle, sharp teeth, long bristles around mouth. Male forehead has pronounced crest. Older male grows to 8 feet and 600 pounds; younger male from 200 to 400 pounds.

Male (mostly younger) is locally common fall through spring. Loud, gregarious. Can be seen (and heard) on bell buoys and off beaches, especially in central Puget Sound. Feeds mostly on Pacific Hake (which concentrates in Saratoga Passage near Everett), Walleye Pollock, Herring, and squids, but will take salmon and Steelhead concentrated at river mouths; infamous for preying on incoming wild Steelhead in Seattle's Lake Washington Ship Canal.

Breeds on islands off the Mexican and California coasts May and June. In winter male ranges north as far as British Columbia. In 1985 700 to 800 were counted near Everett; increasing numbers seen off Seattle beaches. Often regulates body heat by holding flippers out of water.

California sea lions are the agile trained "seals" of circus acts. Can be viewed in the Seattle and Vancouver aquariums and Tacoma's Point Defiance Park.

■ NORTHERN (Steller) SEA LION
Eumetopius jubatus

Massive size. Tawny head and neck; appears whitish when wet; dark brown below and behind. Mature male has thick neck, yellowish mane. No crest on forehead. Does not bark. Breeding male grows to 10 feet long and can weigh over a ton; 3 times heavier than female. Can be dangerous if approached on land.

Locally common fall through spring in north; rare south of Admiralty Inlet. Sucia Island in the San Juan Islands and Race Rocks off southern Vancouver Island are primary haul-out spots. Breeds June to August on islands off Alaska and as far south as California. Opportunistic feeder. Locally feeds on rockfishes, skates, Pacific Hake, Sablefish, Pacific Halibut, salmon, squids, and octopuses. Angers commercial fishermen by damaging nets and netted fish.

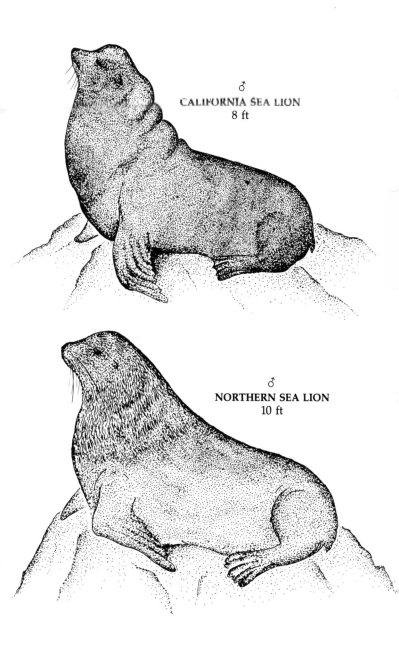

♂
CALIFORNIA SEA LION
8 ft

♂
NORTHERN SEA LION
10 ft

■■■Cetaceans

Order Cetacea

(Whales, Dolphins, and Porpoises)

Have evolved into totally marine mammals over past 65 million years; even give birth at sea. Nostrils moved back to dorsal surface for breathing at water surface. Fur replaced by thick layer of insulative blubber (a few hairs remain on snout). Forelegs evolved into flippers; rear legs disappeared. Long tail ends in broad, muscular fluke, which moves up and down to propel (rather than sideways as in fishou).

Toothed whales (*Suborder* Odontoceti) range in size from sperm whale to small dolphins and porpoises. Few to many teeth. Single blowhole. Use sophisticated sonar to communicate among themselves (whistles) and to hunt (clicks). About 80 species in 6 families.

Baleen whales (*Suborder* Mysticeti) engulf schools of small prey, sieving water through a curtain of fringed cartilage (baleen), which replaces teeth. Nine species in 3 families.

■■Rorquals (Fin-whales)

Family Balaenopteridae

Include humpback and 5 similarly shaped species of *Balaenoptera*.

■MINKE WHALE

Balaenoptera acutorostrata

Solitary. Sexes similar. Similar in shape to the blue whale but a third the length. Dorsal fin is crescent-shaped and set well back on body. Head is flat, narrow, and pointed. Paired blowholes on rear of head. Body is dark gray above; white below. White band on pectoral fin not easily seen. Accordian folds allow throat to expand greatly as the Minke gulps great masses of water and prey. Smallest North American baleen whale. To 30 feet.

Seen in Strait of Juan de Fuca or around San Juan or Canadian Gulf islands. About a dozen in summer, a few remain year-round. Feeds in bays or near shallow banks on small schooling fishes, or rises up to engulf Herring balls (lunge feeding). Shows back and dorsal fin, then dives (without showing tail flukes) for 5 to 10 minutes. Rarely breeches. Changes course unpredictably while underwater.

■■Gray Whale

Family Eschrichtiidae

■GRAY WHALE

Eschrichtius robustus

Narrow, triangular head tilts downward from paired blowholes; covered with white patches and barnacles. Lacks dorsal fin; back has wavy ridge with series of knobs. Medium-sized flippers. Uniform gray color. Female to 45 feet; male slightly smaller.

Migrates up West Coast April and June to northern Pacific and arctic feeding grounds; down coast November and December to breeding lagoons in Baja California. Strays into inland waters during migration—breeders feed in Strait of Juan de Fuca in summer; non-breeders recorded in all seasons, may remain for lengthy periods. Restricted to shallow water. Squirts water from side of mouth to stir up mud; strains out amphipods, worms, clams, and small bottom fishes. Vulnerable to toxics in mud. Almost exterminated by coastal whaling but has recovered after a half-century of protection.

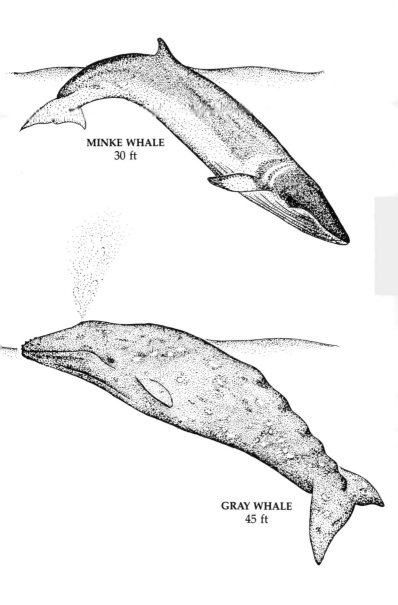

MINKE WHALE
30 ft

GRAY WHALE
45 ft

■■■Dolphins
Family Delphinidae

Conical, pointed teeth (porpoise family has spade-shaped teeth). About 40 species; most oceanic. Orca is only species common east of Port Angeles, but in summer **Pacific white-sided dolphin, short-finned pilot whale,** and (rarely) **Risso's dolphin** sometimes follow squids into Strait of Juan de Fuca. In 1986 a pod of 12 **false killer whales was seen in southern** Puget Sound, the first sighting in half a century.

■ ORCA (Killer Whale)
Orcinus orca

Distinctive dorsal fin: mature male's is triangular, to 6 feet tall; female's and juvenile's is curved, to under 3 feet. Robust body; slender tail with wide fluke. Large, paddle-shaped flippers. Blunt snout. Large mouth and teeth. Distinctive black and white pattern. Jet black above with gray saddle behind dorsal fin; oval white patch behind eye; white underparts extend in a lobe up side. Largest dolphin. Male to 30 feet, 7 tons. Female to 25 feet.

Found worldwide. About 250 resident around Vancouver Island, one of world's densest concentrations. Local "southern community" consists of 3 pods (extended families): J-Pod (18 whales), K-Pod (17), and L-Pod (46). Small pods of "transients" also move through inland waters. Each community of pods has its own distinctive "dialect" of clicks, creaks, and whistles.

In summer J-Pod and K-Pod are common in the inland waters; L-Pod less so. J-Pod makes periodic summer forays into inner Puget Sound (the others occasionally). In winter J-Pod remains in inland waters while K- and L-pods move to outer coast of Vancouver Island. Transient pods pass silently through the area, feeding on seals and other marine mammals. Local orca feed on salmon, rockfishes, cods, and squids.

Combining sight and sonar, formidable intelligence, cooperative hunting, great strength, and speed (up to 25 knots), this largest of dolphins is the ultimate marine predator (though no recorded hostilities toward humans) and most exuberant of marine animals. Pods feed and travel (up to 100 miles daily) during night as well as day.

Male matures sexually in early teens but does not reach full growth until late teens. Starting in midteens, female gives birth no more than once every 3 years.

From 1966 to 1976 orca pods were chased and captured locally for marine amusement parks; a third of local residents were removed or died in the process. Populations have partly recovered since the practice was banned in local waters. Studied in the wild by Friday Harbor's Whale Museum, which also runs summer wildlife cruises and Whale School.

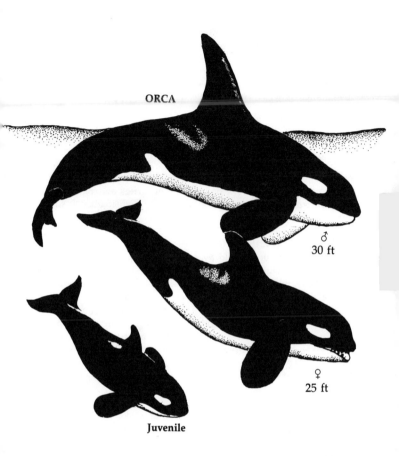

ORCA

♂
30 ft

♀
25 ft

Juvenile

■■ Porpoises
Family Phocoenidae

Told from dolphins by their small, spade-shaped (not conical) teeth. Six species worldwide, 2 in eastern Pacific.

■ DALL'S PORPOISE
Phocoenoides dalli

Robust black body with large white oval patch on sides; white on tips of triangular dorsal fin and small flukes. Small pointed head with small mouth. At distance told by great speed (to 30 knots) and by "rooster tail" plume of water thrown up in wake. When feeding swims in circles, rolling slowly; tail bends 90 degrees before submerging (Indians called it "broken back"). Length to 7 feet.

Seen year-round in pods of a few to a dozen individuals. Common in Strait of Juan de Fuca, San Juan and Canadian Gulf islands, and Admiralty Inlet. Rides bow waves of ferries and powerboats. Feeds on squids and small schooling fishes. High-frequency sonar. Often tangles and drowns in nylon gill nets.

■ HARBOR PORPOISE
Phocoena phocoena

Shy and inconspicuous. Told by small size; small, triangular dorsal fin; and lack of white markings. Small rounded head. Dark gray or brown above; white below. Light grayish area from belly extends up sides to above flipper. Length to 6 feet.

Seen singly or in small pods. Formerly common throughout the area; now rare in southern Puget Sound, perhaps due to drownings in nylon fishing nets. Most seem to move seaward in winter. Feeds on squids, octopuses, Herring, and other small schooling fishes.

■■■ Carnivores
Order Carnivora

■■ Mustelids
Family Mustelidae

Family includes weasels, otters, skunks, and minks. **Sea otter,** found on outer coast, is only truly marine member of this family, but **mink** makes regular forays to intertidal areas, and **river otter** commonly lives at edge of sea.

■ RIVER OTTER
Lutra canadensis

Weasel shape, but much larger. Brown, sleek fur. Active, playful. Unlike sea otter never floats on back. Grows to over 4 feet (including tail) and to over 30 pounds.

Common along all local shores, except near cities. Lives on streams and marshes but is equally tolerant of salt water. Slithers through shallows alone, in pairs, or in families; hunts crabs, fishes, shrimps, and young seabirds. The distinctive dog-sized scat seen on drift logs and boulders, especially where small streams enter salt water, often consists entirely of tiny crab exoskeletons. Slides seen on grassy banks where otters enter the water.

DALL'S PORPOISE
7 ft

HARBOR PORPOISE
6 ft

RIVER OTTER
4 ft

BIRDS

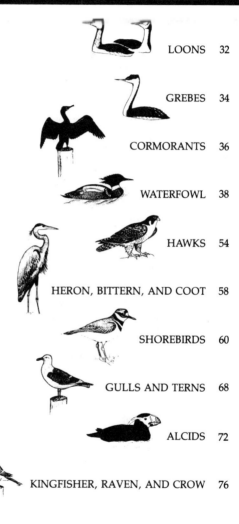

▇▇▇ Loons   *Family* Gaviidae   (*Order* Gaviiformes)

Diving birds, almost helpless on land; leave the water only to nest. Webbed feet; legs set far back on body. Heavy boned; float low in the water. Hunchbacked flight profile. Breed on northern lakes. Mostly silent in winter. Bill is long, narrow, and sharply pointed. Red eyes. Sexes similar.

▇ COMMON LOON   *Gavia immer*

In winter told from other loons by thin white circle around eye and by lack of sharp contrast on neck. Holds head level. **Winter:** Dull brown above; front of neck and lower face are white. Gray bill. **Summer:** Distinctive diagonal green band around striped neck; white spots on back. Dark head with red eye and black bill. Yodels mostly on inland nesting lakes.

Common fall through spring. Strong flier but runs on water to take off. Usually dives when disturbed. Dives for flounders, Herring, sculpins, and other medium to small fishes; also small crustaceans: amphipods, shrimps, and crabs.

The rare **Yellow-billed Loon** (*Gavia adamsii*) has similar summer plumage, but bill is yellow and slightly upturned. In winter browner above than Common Loon; dark spot behind eye.

▇ RED-THROATED LOON   *Gavia stellata*

Winter: Resembles Common Loon but much smaller; sharper contrast between white cheek and grayish nape. Told from other loons by its straight neck held erect; slender upturned bill; spotted brownish back. Head and bill upturned even in flight. **Summer:** Head and back are gray with vertical red neck patch; black-and-white stripes on back of neck. Back is dark brown.

Seen fall through spring, especially in San Juan and Canadian Gulf islands. Dives for flounder and Sand Lance; also eats mussels, crabs, shrimps, and amphipods. Prefers shallow water. Takes off more easily than heavier Common Loon. Call is a low moan.

▇ PACIFIC (Arctic) LOON   *Gavia pacifica*

Winter: Uniformly dark back contrasts with white front. Told from Common Loon by smaller size, from Red-throated Loon by horizontal head posture and darker back. **Summer:** Head and back of neck are handsome gray. Front of neck has rectangular dark patch over black-and-white stripes; white patch below. Back has white spots. Dark to waterline.

Common fall through spring, especially north. Dives (with higher kick than other loons) in tide rips for schooling fishes.

COMMON LOON
L 24 in   W 58 in

Summer

Winter

RED-THROATED LOON
L 17 in   W 44 in

Winter

Summer

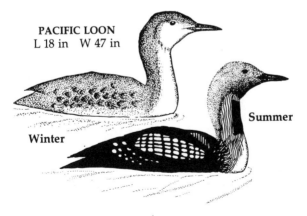

PACIFIC LOON
L 18 in   W 47 in

Summer

Winter

Grebes   *Family* Podicipedidae   (*Order* Podicipediformes)
Diving birds with flat lobes on toes. Legs set far back. Thin, sharp
bills; distinctive foreheads. Dive for small fishes and shrimps. Weak
flyers with short wings; run on water to become airborne. Head held
low in flight but less so than loons. Winter mainly on salt water;
migrate inland to breed on marshes. Sexes similar.

WESTERN GREBE   *Aechmophorus occidentalis*
Neck is long and slender; white front contrasts with dark back. Flat,
black crown. Bill long and sharp; greenish yellow. Red eye surrounded by dark feathers. Plumage similar year-round. Largest local
grebe.

Common fall through spring, often in large concentrations. A
few nonbreeding birds remain in summer. Courtship display includes head bobbing and spectacular pair dance on water. Dives to
spear sculpins, Herring, Shiner Perch, and Surf Smelt.

RED-NECKED GREBE   *Podiceps grisegena*
Medium size. Neck is shorter and stockier than Western Grebe's, but
longer and straighter than Horned Grebe's. Black eye. Stocky yellow
bill. **Winter:** Flattop head profile with dark crown. Straight, erect
neck. White cheeks contrast with gray neck and upper face; dark
above. **Summer:** Brick red neck; gray cheeks outlined in white. Dark
crown and back. Reddish below.

Common spring and fall migrant; winter resident. Feeds singly
or in small flocks. Dives for Stickleback, Herring, sculpins, amphipods, and shrimps.

HORNED GREBE   *Podiceps auritus*
Small. Red eye. **Winter:** White on cheek extends to back of head. Dark
crown, nape, and back contrast with white cheek, neck, and breast.
Summer: Thin, golden "horns" above dark, puffy cheeks. Brick red
neck and sides; dark back.

Common fall through spring. Often seen near docks and seawalls diving for small fishes and crustaceans. Leaps up to begin dive.

EARED GREBE   *Podiceps nigricollis*
Similar in size to Horned Grebe but has thinner neck; in winter has
darker cheeks, less contrast on neck; rides higher in water and leaps
higher before dive. In summer has wide golden fan behind red eye;
black neck and back; red flanks.

An uncommon winter resident; usually seen in protected bays.

WESTERN GREBE
L 18 in   W 40 in

RED-NECKED GREBE
L 13 in   W 32 in

Summer

Winter

HORNED GREBE
L 9 in   W 24 in

Winter

Summer

EARED GREBE
L 9 in   W 23 in

Winter

■■■ Cormorants

Family Phalacrocoracidae
(*Order* Pelecaniformes)

Large diving birds with hooked, serrated bill for grasping fish. Bill held uptilted while swimming. Colorful, bare facial skin. Webbed feet used for propulsion underwater. Heavy bodied; float low in water and slow to take off. Wary. Silent except in breeding colonies. Often seen on rocks or pilings holding wings out to dry. Adult plumage mostly similar year round. Sexes similar.

■ PELAGIC CORMORANT

Phalacrocorax pelagicus

In breeding season has conspicuous white patch on flanks and white plumes on side of neck. Slender bill with swollen tip. In flight long tail is conspicuous (same length as neck and head). Adult is uniformly black with greenish gloss; double crest visible. Red facial skin. Immature is dark brown. Smallest and thinnest of our 3 species.

Common resident. Dives in tidal rips for Herring, bottom fish, and crustaceans. About 1,000 pairs breed locally, usually on steep, rocky cliffs. Carries seaweed for nest.

■ DOUBLE-CRESTED CORMORANT

Phalacrocorax auritus

Orange throat patch. In flight kinked neck is conspicuous. White breeding crests small and inconspicuous. Adult plumage is uniformly black. Immature is dark brown above, brownish breast and front of neck; darker belly.

Most common of our 3 local species. Occurs year-round. Breeds on rocky islets in and near Strait of Juan de Fuca; seen carrying large nest sticks. Dives over sandy or gravelly bottoms to depths of 60 feet for Stickleback, sculpins, and juvenile salmonids.

■ BRANDT'S CORMORANT

Phalacrocorax penicillatus

In flight tail is noticeably short, head is large, and neck straight. Adult is uniformly black. Immature is dark brown with large, pale Y on breast. **Summer:** Throat patch is bright blue surrounded by dull yellow feathers. Breeding birds have thin, white plumes on upper neck and back.

Common winter resident. Nonbreeders locally common in summer. Breeds on outer coast. Dives, sometimes in groups, for schools of Herring and other small fishes; to depths of up to 160 feet. Prefers tidal rips.

PELAGIC CORMORANT
L 22 in   W 40 in

**DOUBLE-CRESTED
CORMORANT**
L 27 in   W 50 in

BRANDT'S CORMORANT
L 29 in   W 50 in

▄▄▄ Waterfowl   *Family* Anatidae   (*Order* Anseriformes)

Waterfowl include swans, geese, and ducks. Most have long necks; all have webbed feet and narrow, pointed wings. Bills are flattened and have serrated edges to strain aquatic plants or small animals from the water. Young waterfowl are precocious; walk, feed, and swim within hours of hatching. All North American waterfowl belong to the large family Anatidae, which is divided into 8 tribes (subfamilies).

▄▄ Swans   *Tribe* Cygnini

Our largest, heaviest, and longest-necked waterfowl. Feed on shore grasses and tip for aquatic vegetation.

▄ TUNDRA (Whistling) SWAN   *Cygnus columbianus*

Conspicuously large. At rest tends to hold long, slender neck up erect from breast. Concave, black bill tapers to point near eye and has yellow "tear" spot at base. Adult plumage is uniformly white. Immature is light gray; bill pinkish with gray tip.

Common, early spring migrant on shallow bays. About 200 winter on salt marshes near Skagit and Nooksack rivers. Feeds on aquatic plants, waste crops, and small mollusks. Call is similar to Canada Goose, but higher pitched.

▄ TRUMPETER SWAN   *Cygnus buccinator*

At distance is difficult to tell from Tundra Swan, but somewhat larger. Closer up, bill profile is straighter, black area is wider near eye, and lacks yellow spot. At rest tends to hold neck kinked at base. Adult all-white, but head and belly sometimes stained by tannins in marsh water. Immature is gray.

Rare on salt water, but in winter sometimes seen on sloughs, especially Skagit River Delta. Call is low honk followed by 3 high-pitched notes.

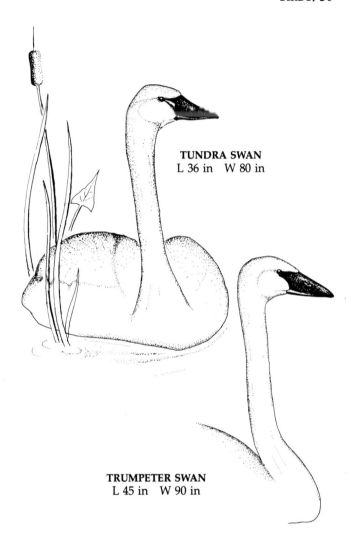

TUNDRA SWAN
L 36 in   W 80 in

TRUMPETER SWAN
L 45 in   W 90 in

■ Geese
Tribe Anserini

Large plump birds with medium-to-long necks and short, strong legs. Graze on grasses and aquatic plants. Strong fliers; migrate in noisy, ragged V-shaped flocks. Sexes similar.

■ CANADA GOOSE
Branta canadensis

Large, familiar goose with familiar braying call. Black head and neck; white cheek patch. Dark brown back; light brown breast and sides; white belly. Prefers to migrate along fresh water or outer seacoast. When migrating locally, feeds on Sea Lettuce and salt marsh plants.

■ SNOW GOOSE
Chen caerulescens

Adult is pure white except for black tips of wing. Pink bill with black patch on lower mandible; pink feet. Immature is mottled brownish gray above with black wing tips; dark bill; light cheek patches.

Common fall and spring migrant; abundant on the Skagit and Stillaguamish river deltas in winter. Feeds on Sea Lettuce, Eelgrass, salt marsh plants, and farm grains.

■ BRANT (Black Brant)
Branta bernicla

Dark, stocky. Neck relatively short for a goose. Adult has white neck ring below head. Bill, feet, and plumage are dark, except for white "necklace," light patch on flanks, and white belly. Immature is all black.

Common spring and fall migrant; winter resident on shallow bays. Padilla Bay hosts up to 10,000 (down ⅔ since early 1970s). Feeds in shallows and mud flats on Eelgrass and Sea Lettuce.

The **Greater White-fronted Goose** (*Anser albifrons*) is occasionally seen flying overhead during migration or wintering on shallow bays and salt marshes. Adult has light-tipped, pink bill ringed with white; orange feet. Dark gray-brown above; light breast with black streaks. Immature lacks breast streaks.

CANADA GOOSE
L 25 in   W 68 in

SNOW GOOSE
L 19 in   W 59 in

BRANT
L 17 in   W 46 in

◼ Dabbling Ducks   *Tribe* Anatini

Feed on shallow-water plants by tipping head down, tail up. Strong fliers; can take off vertically. Have "speculum" (brightly colored wing patch) on inner trailing edge of upper wing surface. Males of most species assume drab "eclipse plumage" for a few weeks after breeding. **Male:** Denotes colorful fall-through-spring plumage. **Female:** Denotes female, juvenile, and male eclipse plumage.

◼ MALLARD   *Anas platyrhynchos*

Blue speculum with white border. Orange legs. Tail bordered with white. **Male:** Metallic green head separated from chestnut breast by narrow white ring. Yellow bill; black tail. **Female:** Mottled brown. Dark line through eye. Orange bill with dark tip.

Abundant resident, especially in estuarine bays; peak in late fall. Feeds in shallow water on variety of plants, crustaceans, and mollusks.

◼ NORTHERN SHOVELER   *Anas clypeata*

Long, shovel-shaped bill; short neck. Metallic green speculum bordered by white; large blue wing patch. **Male:** Green head with black bill. White breast. Rusty sides and belly; vertical white bar before black tail. Immature has gray head with white crescent before eye. **Female:** Gray and orange bill. Mottled brown head and body.

Common winter resident (occasional breeder) in shallow bays; prefers fresh water. Strains water for amphipods and other small animals.

◼ NORTHERN PINTAIL   *Anas acuta*

Male: Long, slender, black tail plume. Brown head and nape. Front of neck is white with thin line extending up nape. Gray back and sides. Speculum brown and green bordered by yellow and white. **Female:** Mottled gray-brown. Lacks tail plumes. Muted speculum. Both sexes have gray bill, eye, and feet.

Common spring and fall migrant and winter resident (occasional breeder). On salt water feeds on mollusks and crustaceans; on fresh water, mostly on plants.

◼ AMERICAN WIGEON   *Anas americana*

Large white patch in front of green speculum (female's is muted). Bill is bluish gray tipped with black. **Male:** White crown gives "baldpate" nickname. Rest of head and upper neck are speckled gray with metallic green patch behind eye. Brown back. Rusty breast and sides; white belly; black tail. **Female:** Finely speckled gray head; brown body.

Abundant winter resident in sheltered bays. Large, wary flocks. Dabbles for Eelgrass, Sea Lettuce, and other seaweeds; also grazes on grasses. Steals food from American Coot.

The **Eurasian (European) Wigeon** (*Anas penelope*) sometimes seen with American. Male has yellow crown and rusty face; lacks green face patch. Gray sides. Female's head is brown, not gray.

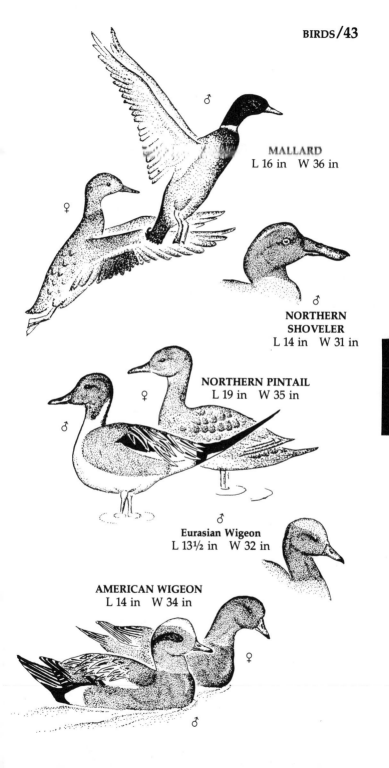

MALLARD
L 16 in W 36 in

♂

♀

NORTHERN SHOVELER
L 14 in W 31 in

♂

NORTHERN PINTAIL
L 19 in W 35 in

♀

♂

♂

Eurasian Wigeon
L 13½ in W 32 in

AMERICAN WIGEON
L 14 in W 34 in

♀

♂

■**GREEN-WINGED TEAL** *Anas crecca*

Smallest dabbler. Dark bill and eye. **Male:** Vertical white stripe on gray side near breast. Rusty head with iridescent green patch behind eye. Brown back and wings. Bright green speculum. Speckled tan breast. Yellow under dark tail. **Female:** Mottled brown. Told from other teals by small bill and white underwing coverts.

Common winter resident (occasional breeder) in estuaries. Feeds in shallow, brackish water on Eelgrass, sedges, and other vegetation.

■**Bay Ducks (Pochards)** *Tribe* Aythyini

Diving ducks; swim underwater and feed more on aquatic animals than do dabbling ducks. Run along water to become airborne. Calls are short, low croaks.

■**GREATER SCAUP** *Aythya marila*

Female has white face ring. Both sexes have broad white trailing edge of wing; gray bill with black "nail" at tip. Yellow eye. Told from Lesser Scaup by more rounded head and larger bill. **Male:** Dark, iridescent head has greenish cast. Black breast. Dark gray above, light gray below; black tail. **Female:** Front of face is white around bill. Uniformly brown body; white belly.

Common spring and fall migrant and winter resident in sheltered bays, often with Bufflehead and Scoters. Feeds on small clams, crabs, Sea Lettuce, and Eelgrass; Herring eggs in spring.

The similar **Lesser Scaup** (*Aythya affinis*) is often seen with Greater Scaup. Told by more pointed crown and smaller bill. Male's head has purple cast rather than green. Smaller white patch on wing. Bill tip has smaller "nail." Prefers fresh water.

■**CANVASBACK** *Aythya valisineria*

Stout, concave, uniformly black bill descends from sloping forehead. Pointed head. Long neck. No wing patch. **Male:** Chestnut head contrasts with black breast. Light gray sides and back; black tail. **Female:** Light brown head; darker brown breast; lighter tail.

Locally common winter resident. Prefers open water of bays. Feeds on aquatic plants, small fishes, and mussels.

■**REDHEAD** *Aythya americana*

Plumage patterns similar to Canvasback. Told by shorter neck, rounder head; darker back and sides; gray bill with black tip separated by white. No speculum.

Uncommon. Prefers fresh water, but sometimes seen in salt marshes. Feeds mostly on aquatic plants.

**GREEN-WINGED
TEAL**
L 10½ in   W 24 in

GREATER SCAUP
L 13 in   W 31 in

REDHEAD
L 14 in   W 33 in

CANVASBACK
L 15 in   W 34 in

■ Sea ducks

Tribe Mergini

Short-necked ducks; dive for mussels and clams. In winter often seen in small groups close to seawalls and marinas.

■ COMMON GOLDENEYE

Bucephala clangula

Male: Large, round white spot below and in front of golden eye. Shiny dark green head. White neck and lower body. Large white wing patch on black wing. In flight shows bold black-and-white pattern on back and wings. **Female:** Reddish brown head with golden eye. Wide, white neck ring, belly, and speculum; otherwise gray. Both sexes have dark bill; female's tipped with orange in spring.

Widespread spring and fall migrant; winter resident. Found in sheltered inlets and near seawalls. Dives up to 20 feet for mussels and crabs; picks at intertidal rocks for small prey; feeds on Herring spawn in spring. Fast flyer with whistling wingbeats.

■ BARROW'S GOLDENEYE

Bucephala islandica

Male: White crescent in front of pale yellow eye. Head has purple cast, steep forehead. Darker above than Common Goldeneye. On water shows white "windows" along folded wings; white below except for black line extending from shoulder to waterline. Small, white wing patch crossed by thin, black line. **Female:** Reddish brown head with golden eye, steep forehead. White neck ring, belly, and wing patches; otherwise gray. Bill entirely orange in spring.

Common spring and fall migrant; local winter resident, especially south. Seen in pairs or small flocks. Dives for mussels and crabs; picks small organisms off rocks and pilings. Fast flyer with whistling wingbeats.

■ BUFFLEHEAD

Bucephala albeola

Smallest North American duck. Large, puffy head with steep forehead and small bill. **Male:** Iridescent purple-green head with large, triangular, white patch. Snowy white neck, breast, and belly. In flight shows bold black-and-white pattern on back and wings. **Female:** Dark gray head with thin, white, oval patch behind eye. Gray back and wings; black wing tips and small, white wing patch. Light gray sides; white below.

Spring and fall migrant; common winter resident in sheltered bays. Dives for small mollusks, crustaceans, and small fishes. In spring often seen in flocks close to shore. Courting male darts foreward, bobs head, and displays white crest.

COMMON GOLDENEYE
L 13 in   W 31 in

BARROW'S GOLDENEYE
L 13 in   W 31 in

BUFFLEHEAD
L 10 in   W 24 in

■HARLEQUIN DUCK   *Histrionicus histrionicus*

Chunky duck with striking male plumage. High forehead. Small black bill. **Male:** Bluish gray. White crescent (upper end tinged with red) before dark eye. White spot and thinner crescent on side of head. White streaks (breast pair edged with black) on breast, back, and wings. Rusty sides; black tail. **Female:** Dark brown with tan belly. Three white spots on side of head.

Common on Strait of Juan de Fuca and north; rare south of Admiralty Inlet. Dives for snails, chitons, crabs, and small fishes. Breeds upriver in spring. Males (and a few nonbreeding females) gather in small groups on exposed rocky shores in summer, while females and ducklings float slowly downriver to join males for the winter.

■OLDSQUAW   *Clangula hyemalis*

Yodeling whistle. Male has long, upswept tail plume. Dramatic, variable plumage patterns; only duck with conspicuous winter/summer plumage change. In flight told by white head with short, dark wings. On water sides are white to waterline in all plumages. **Male/Winter:** White body with two-tone brown cheek patch. Dark band on lower breast. Wings dark brown with tan wing patch. In flight shows black streak down back to tail plume. Gray, elongated shoulder feathers. Orange ring on brown bill. **Male/Summer:** Dark brown except for light gray eye patch, sides, and belly. **Female/Winter:** Dark crown and back; otherwise white. Lacks cheek patch and tail plume. **Female/Summer:** Dark above; side of head and neck are white with brown cheek patch.

Locally common winter resident in north; rare south of Admiralty Inlet. Dives to 100 feet for mussels, amphipods, crabs, shrimps, and small fishes.

HARLEQUIN DUCK
L 12 in   W 26 in

♂

♀

OLDSQUAW
L 15 in   W 30 in
Summer

Winter

♂

♂

Winter

♀

Summer

♀

■SURF SCOTER
Melanitta perspicillata

Male: White patch on forehead and back of neck. Large, conspicuous bill is orange with black spot near base surrounded by white. Body and wings are all-black. **Female:** Dark brown, with 2 white cheek patches.

Common spring and fall migrant; abundant winter resident. Some remain through summer. Dives for mussels and crabs; uses wings and feet for swim underwater.

■WHITE-WINGED SCOTER
Melanitta fusca

White wing patch (usually visible when swimming). **Male:** Slender, white eye patch and large, white wing patch; otherwise all-black. Black bump at base of orange bill. **Female:** Two white cheek patches; touch of orange on bill. Dark brown above; lighter below. Larger than other 2 scoters.

Common spring and fall migrant; locally abundant winter resident. Some nonbreeders remain through summer. Sometimes seen in large rafts but more often in small groups. Dives for mussels, crabs, and clams; Herring eggs in spring.

■BLACK SCOTER
Melanitta nigra

Male: All-black except for bright orange bump at base of bill. **Female:** All-brown except for large, creamy patch on cheek and front of neck.

Uncommon winter resident; often seen with other scoters. In spring male displays to females with a series of head bobs with whistles; presses bill to breast; finishes with a fast run and breast slide.

SURF SCOTER
L 14 in   W 33 in

♀

♂

**WHITE-WINGED
SCOTER**
L 16 in   W 38 in

♀

♂

BLACK SCOTER
L 14 in   W 33 in

♀

♂

■RED-BREASTED MERGANSER · *Mergus serrator*

Shaggy double crests on head. Male wears a "vest." Thin, serrated, bright orange bill; orange eyes and feet. **Male:** Dark green crested head. White neck; brown, speckled breast. Dark back; gray sides; dingy belly; brown tail. White inner wing. **Female:** Reddish crested head. Dark face. Whitish front of neck and breast, but less contrast than female Common Merganser. Gray above; lighter belly. Smaller white wing patch bordered with black.

Common spring and fall migrant; winter resident. Dives for small fishes; Herring eggs in spring. Male courtship display consists of head dips, neck thrusts, and chases, often near shore.

■HOODED MERGANSER · *Lophodytes cucullatus*

Small body; small, thin bill. Long, flattened crest. **Male:** Black head with large, white crest outlined in black. High forehead. Yellow eye. Black neck contrasts with white breast. Black back; rusty sides. **Female:** Tawny crest; otherwise brown above; white belly.

Common in San Juan and Canadian Gulf islands; uncommon elsewhere. Prefers fresh water, but found on bays and inlets in winter. Dives in sheltered water for fishes and crustaceans.

■COMMON MERGANSER · *Mergus merganser*

Long, bright orange bill. White breast. **Male:** Shiny, dark green head; lacks crest. White neck, breast, and sides. White inner wings; brown outer. **Female:** Reddish, slightly crested head contrasts sharply with white chin and breast (more so than female Red-breasted Merganser). Otherwise gray. Small, white wing patch with heavy black border.

Locally common fall and spring migrant. Seen in large flocks in winter. Dives for small fishes.

■Stiff-tailed Ducks · *Tribe* Oxyurini

Only one northern species. Dive (or slowly sink) like grebes.

■RUDDY DUCK · *Oxyura jamaicensis*

Stiff, brown tail often upturned. Short, stubby body with short neck. **Male:** Blue bill. Black "cap." Large, white cheek patch. Ruddy (rusty) body. Short, rounded brown wings with darker wing patch. In winter similar to female, but cheek patch stays bright white. **Female:** Gray bill. Horizontal brown line through whitish cheek patch. Dark brown above; lighter below.

Uncommon winter resident, scattered around protected bays and salt marshes. Prefers fresh water. Mostly silent. Dives for seaweeds, some small mollusks, and crustaceans. Flies low over water with fast wingbeats. Dives when disturbed.

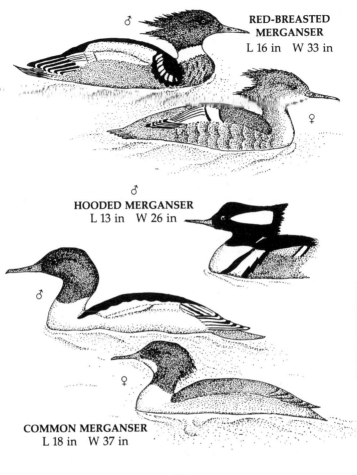

♂

**RED-BREASTED
MERGANSER**
L 16 in   W 33 in

♀

♂

HOODED MERGANSER
L 13 in   W 26 in

♂

♀

COMMON MERGANSER
L 18 in   W 37 in

♂
RUDDY DUCK
L 11 in   W 23 in
Winter

■Hawks and Eagles

Family Accipitridae
(Order Falconiformes)

Diurnal birds of prey with hooked bills and strong talons. Female usually larger than male.

■OSPREY (Fish Hawk)
Pandion haliaetus

Long, bent wings with bold black "wrist" marks. White face with dark line through red eye. Dark brown above; white below. Underwings are white with dark brown stripes, wrist marks, and tips. Tail barred.

Locally common fall and spring migrant; summer resident. Hovers from heights and dives, talons first, for large fish. Bent wings allow vertical lift-off from water. Grasps fish with specially adapted talons; carries it back to perch or nest. Nest is large tangle of sticks high up in snag along rivers or estuarine beach. Returns to same nest annually. Vocal near nest. Call is series of shrill whistles.

■NORTHERN HARRIER (Marsh Hawk)
Circus cyaneus

Recognized by slender build and conspicuous white rump; low, slow, tilting flight with wings held in shallow V. **Male:** Gray above; white below with reddish spots. Dark-tipped wings. "Barred" tail. **Female:** Larger than male. Brown body with streaking on breast. Darker bars and streaking on wings and tail. Immature is tinged with cinnamon below.

Common salt marsh resident. Often perches on ground. Preys on voles (field mice); also takes ducks, shorebirds, frogs, and other small animals. Hunts by sound and sight: owllike facial mask directs sound to sensitive ears. Nest is mound of marsh vegetation or tall prairie grasses.

■RED-TAILED HAWK
Buteo jamaicensis

In flight adult told by reddish tail, "belly band," and broad, rounded wings. Plumage variable: dark brown above; dark to light below with darker band across belly. Wings are whitish with dark primaries and leading edge. Tail of adult is red above, pink below with very narrow, dark band near end. Tail of immature is brown and finely barred.

Common resident of marshes and open areas near beach. Perches in trees, telephone poles, or fences. Soars. Feeds on rodents, rabbits, and other small animals. High-soaring, conspicuous courtship flight. Nests are large and visible; 40 to 80 feet high, often in cottonwood trees (conifers in San Juan Islands). Call is distinctive, harsh descending scream.

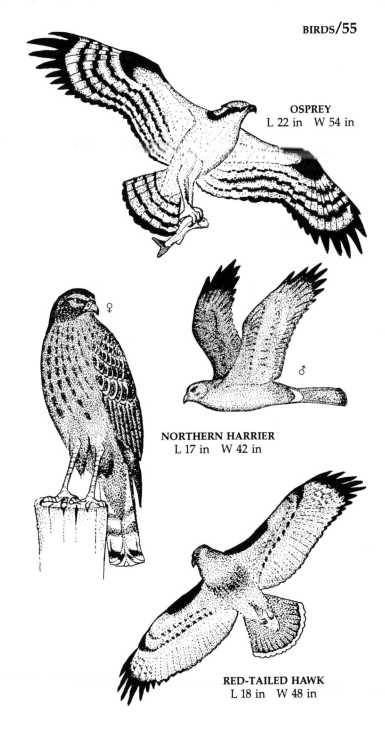

OSPREY
L 22 in   W 54 in

♀

♂

NORTHERN HARRIER
L 17 in   W 42 in

RED-TAILED HAWK
L 18 in   W 48 in

■ BALD EAGLE   *Haliaeetus leucocephalus*

Adult is dark brown with white head and tail. Hooked, bright yellow bill. Wings held straight out when soaring. Immature is mottled with white; head gradually whitens during first 3 years; bill is brown with touch of yellow at base. In flight juvenile is told from golden eagle by longer head, shorter tail, and white mottling.

Locally common resident. Seen perching upright on snags over looking water. Preys on fishes and marine birds. Robs osprey and gulls of fish; scavanges on spawned salmon and beach carrion. Each pair builds 2 or 3 nests on territory but uses only 1 in any given year. Cry is unexpectedly high-pitched for such a large bird.

■ Falcons   *Family* Falconidae   (*Order* Falconiformes)

Fast fliers; hunt smaller birds. Wings are long and narrow; bent at "wrist."

■ MERLIN (Pigeon Hawk)   *Falco columbarius*

Male: Face is striped and has thin vertical line below eye. Dark gray above; finely striped below. **Female:** Similar pattern but brown. Both sexes have strongly barred tail. Told from larger Peregrine Falcon by tail pattern and lack of facial "helmet"; from smaller kestrel by lack of bold facial bars and lack of rusty plumage.

Seen on tideflats and salt marshes in winter. Dives on shorebirds and small perching birds.

■ PEREGRINE FALCON   *Falco peregrinus*

Narrow, pointed wings. Adult has dark "helmet." Dark above; light below with fine barring. Immature is darker with a light forehead.

Uncommon but spectacular migrant. Follows flocks of migrating shorebirds; "stoops" (dives at high speeds) on ducks and shorebirds. Seen perched on beach pilings and tall snags. Some overwinter. Breeding pairs recently reestablished in north.

MERLIN
L 12 in   W 23 in

♂
PEREGRINE FALCON
L 15 in   W 40 in

BALD EAGLE
L 32 in   W 80 in

▰▰ Herons   *Family* Ardeidae   (*Order* Ciconiiformes)

The family includes herons and bitterns. The order includes 2 other families of long-legged wading birds: ibises and spoonbills; and wood storks.

▰ GREAT BLUE HERON   *Ardea herodias*

Large size. Long, slender legs. Long, sharp bill. In flight folds back neck. **Adult:** White face; black stripe extends from above eye to slender black plume. Gray body and wings; front of neck and breast are spotted. Breeding adult has long gray plume feathers on breast and back. **Immature:** Brownish gray where adults are bluish gray; lacks head plume.

Familiar, year-round resident of bays and salt marshes; also seen hunting on rocky coasts. Stalks or stands, and then strikes at a variety of shallow-water fishes, frogs, snakes, and other small aquatic animals. Nests in treetop colonies called rookeries.

▰ AMERICAN BITTERN   *Botaurus lentiginosus*

Large, striped body. Sharp, stout bill. Bold "sideburn" (black stripe on side of upper neck). Upright "freeze" posture. Distinctive spring call. Brown back and wings with blackish flight feathers. White throat. Brown spots below. Greenish legs.

Common, but elusive, in cattail marshes. Most active at dusk and dawn. More apt to be heard than seen: spring call is loud, pumplike *gung-ga-goonk*. When disturbed freezes with bill pointed upward.

▰▰ Rails   *Family* Rallidae   (*Order* Gruiformes)

The large family includes rails, gallinules, and coots. The order includes 2 other families of wading birds: cranes and limpkins.

▰ AMERICAN COOT   *Fulica americana*

White bill and forehead "shield" contrasts with dark head and body. Red eye. Uniformly black above. Short tail. Long, greenish yellow toes with lobes on sides.

Locally common resident. Seen primarily in salt-marsh sloughs, fresh marshes, and estuarine mud flats. Feeds on plant matter in shallow water and on edge of land.

**GREAT
BLUE HERON**
L 38 in   W 70 in

**AMERICAN
BITTERN**
L 23 in   W 45 in

AMERICAN COOT
L 12 in   W 25 in

▨ Oystercatchers

Family Haematopodidae
(*Order* Charadriiformes)

One of 5 shorebird families. The large, varied order also includes gulls, terns, and jaegers (*Family* Laridae); and alcids (*Family* Alcidae).

▪ AMERICAN BLACK OYSTERCATCHER

Haematopus bachmani

Long, straight red bill. Dark body. Pink legs. Yellow eye.

On rocky shores, often in pairs. Prys limpets and chitons off rocks; chisels mussels open. Male courtship display is long flights with slow wingbeats, loud calls, and distinctive head-down bow before female. Call (piping) is repeated piercing whistle.

▨ Plovers

Family Charadriidae   (*Order* Charadriiformes)

Medium-to-small ground-nesting shorebirds. Forage in the high intertidal and above tide line in manner of robins. Neck and tail are short. Bill has swelling at tip.

▪ KILLDEER

Charadrius vociferus

Adult has 2 black "collars" (juvenile has single brown band). Brown head with white forehead and eye stripe. Brown back and forewings. White wing stripe; trailing edge of wing is black. Orange rump extends onto black tail edged with white. White below. Thin black bill. Red circle of iris shows around large black pupil. Pinkish legs.

Our most familiar and widespread shorebird. Seen year-round on beaches, marshes, and fields. Feeds on variety of crustaceans, mollusks, marine worms, and insects. Nests on ground; feigns broken wing when disturbed near nest. Call is shrill, repeated *kill-dee*.

▪ SEMIPALMATED PLOVER

Charadrius semipalmatus

Single "collar" and very short neck. **Summer:** Dark head with white on forehead and above eye. Brown back and wings; white wing stripe. White below with dark breast band. Dark tail edged with white. Orange legs. **Winter:** Plumage muted; light brown breast band. White forehead extends above eye. Yellowish legs.

Fairly common spring and fall migrant. Feeds robinlike on intertidal marine worms, mollusks, and crustaceans.

▪ BLACK-BELLIED PLOVER

Pluvialis squatarola

Stout black bill; black legs. In flight told by white rump and black patches under base of wings. Mottled back in winter; black face and breast in summer. Similar **Lesser Golden-Plover** *(Pluvialis dominica)* lacks black underwing and white rump; has smaller bill. **Winter:** Mottled black-and-tan above. Faint white wing stripe. White rump; banded tail. Light band above eye. Mottled gray breast; white belly. **Summer:** Mottled black above. Bold black face, breast, and upper belly edged by sharply contrasting white.

Fairly common spring and fall migrant; locally common winter resident. Small, wary flocks on sheltered beaches and salt marshes. Feeds robinlike on worms, mollusks, and insects.

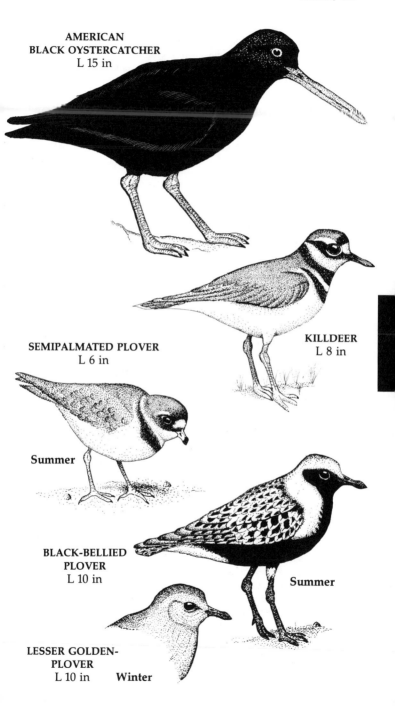

**AMERICAN
BLACK OYSTERCATCHER**
L 15 in

KILLDEER
L 8 in

SEMIPALMATED PLOVER
L 6 in

Summer

**BLACK-BELLIED
PLOVER**
L 10 in

Summer

**LESSER GOLDEN-
PLOVER**
L 10 in   **Winter**

■ **Sandpipers**   *Family* Scolopacidae   (*Order* Charadriiformes)

Large, varied shorebird family. Bills longer, more slender than plovers'. Feathers have pale edging giving plumage mottled look. Most species have distinctive breeding plumage. Sexes usually similar.

■ **WANDERING TATTLER**   *Heteroscelus incanus*

Fairly long, dark, straight and slender bill. Light stripe above eye. Yellowish legs. **Winter:** Gray above. Dusky breast. White belly. **Summer:** Dark above; fine, black crossbarring below.

   Usually seen singly along rocky and cobbly beaches in spring and fall. Bobs head, but less often than smaller Spotted Sandpiper. Feeds on small mollusks, marine worms, and crustaceans.

■ **DUNLIN**   *Calidris alpina*

Longish, dark bill with noticeable droop at tip. Thin white wing stripe. **Winter:** Uniformly gray above, with thin white line above eye. Thin white line on wing. Tip and trailing edge of wing are dark. Light gray breast; white belly. Told from Sanderling by darker color and larger bill; from Western Sandpiper by bill and larger size. **Summer:** Rusty back. Distinctive black belly patch.

   Abundant migrant; common winter resident. Seen in large flocks along beaches and mud flats. White bellies flash as flock flies in unison. Probes water's edge for amphipods, marine worms, and small clams. Call is distinctive *cree*.

■ **SANDERLING**   *Calidris alba*

Small, straight dark bill. Black legs. In winter lightest plumage of any shorebird. In flight told by bold, white wing stripe. Runs along water's edge. **Winter:** Mottled light gray above; snowy white below. White stripe above eye. White wing stripe; black tip and trailing edge of wing. **Summer:** Mottled reddish brown above and on breast. No eye stripe.

   Seen on sandy beaches in spring and late fall; some overwinter with Dunlin and Western Sandpiper. Breeds in high Arctic. Often stops at same beaches year after year. Runs at wave's edge in a line or in small groups, probing for amphipods, marine worms, and small fishes. Also feeds on beach hoppers and flies in beach wrack. Call is sharp *kip, kip*.

■ **WESTERN SANDPIPER**   *Calidris mauri*

No wing stripe. Dark, medium-length bill with slight droop at tip. Told from Least Sandpiper by dark legs and larger size; from Dunlin in winter by smaller size and thinner bill. **Winter:** Grayish brown above with some rust on shoulders. White stripe above eye. White below with some mottling on breast. In flight dark trailing edge of wings; dark line down rump and tail. **Summer:** Rusty back; darker wings. Brown spotting on breast.

   Abundant spring and fall migrant. Seen on tidal mud flats and nearby beaches. Probes in shallow water for amphipods and marine worms.

Summer

WANDERING
TATTLER
L 9 in   W 20 in

Winter

DUNLIN
L 7 in

Winter

SANDERLING
L 6½ in

Winter

WESTERN
SANDPIPER
L 5½ in

■**LEAST SANDPIPER** *Calidris minutilla*
Yellowish legs. Small, thin, straight bill. Found with and similar to Western Sandpiper, but noticeably smaller; more tan on breast; feeds higher up on beach.

Common spring and fall migrant; rare in winter. Seen on mud flats and sand beaches. Feeds on amphipods and marine worms.

■**SPOTTED SANDPIPER** *Actitis macularia*
Head held down. Bobs tail continuously. Flies with stiff, shallow, rapid wingbeats. Feet pink to flesh colored. **Winter:** Dark brown above; white below. White stripe above eye. Short white wing stripe. **Summer:** Adult has dark spots from throat to belly.

Uncommon migrant. A few nest locally near marshes, ponds, and river gravel bars. Feeds on small crustaceans and marine worms on mud flats and in seaweed-covered rocks.

■**BLACK TURNSTONE** *Arenaria melanocephala*
Short, upturned bill. In flight shows bold black-and-white pattern on back and wings. **Winter:** Dusky except for white belly. **Summer:** Darker plumage. White spot at base of bill. White eye stripe.

Seen late summer through spring on rocky beaches; less common south of Admiralty Inlet. Feeds by dislodging limpets and by overturning pebbles and seaweed for crabs and amphipods. Call is loud, high-pitched rattle.

■**RUDDY TURNSTONE** *Arenaria interpres*
Short, slender, upturned bill. Orange legs. **Winter:** Dark above; light below with black V on breast (Black Turnstone has all-gray breast). **Summer:** In flight shows distinctive, complex pattern of rust, white, and black on back and wings. Rusty above; white below with bold, black breast pattern extending up to eye.

Uncommon migrant; prefers outer coast. Feeds as Black Turnstone. Call is rapid series of low, slurred whistles.

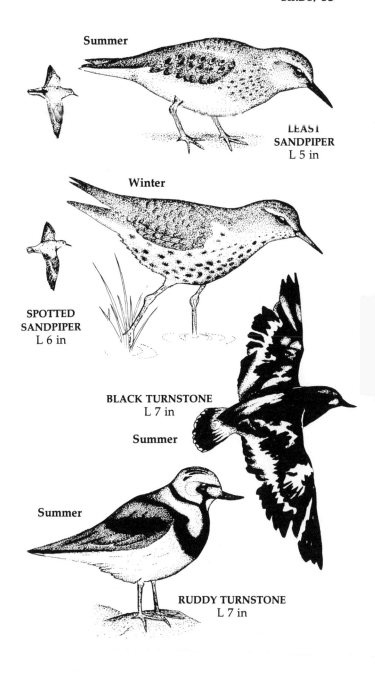

Summer

LEAST
SANDPIPER
L 5 in

Winter

SPOTTED
SANDPIPER
L 6 in

BLACK TURNSTONE
L 7 in

Summer

Summer

RUDDY TURNSTONE
L 7 in

■**LONG-BILLED DOWITCHER**   *Limnodromus scolopaceus*
Very long, straight, dark bill. **Winter:** Grayish brown back and
wings; lighter breast. Dark eye line. White rump extends in V up
back. Finely barred tail. **Summer:** Rustier except for rump. Dark mottling on back; fine stripes below.

Common spring and fall migrant in north; less common south.
Seen in salt marshes; prefers freshwater marshes. Call is sharp,
high-pitched *keek keek*.

The **Short-billed Dowitcher** (*Limnodromus griseus*) is a bit smaller
and has somewhat shorter bill. Prefers salt marshes. Flanks spotted,
rather than barred. Both species seen in salt marshes and tideflats in
spring and fall; best distinguished by calls. Probes shallows for
marine worms, crustaceans, and small clams. Call is mellow *tu-tu-tu*
in rapid series.

■**WHIMBREL**   *Numenius phaeopus*
Very long, dark, down-curved bill. Black-and-white striped crown.
Grayish brown above; lighter below except for rusty underwings.
Dark spots on neck, breast, and wings. Finely barred tail. Plumage
similar year-round.

Common spring and fall migrant; some overwinter. Seen on
tideflats, salt marshes, and offshore rocks. Probes for mud shrimps,
crabs, and worms. Call is repeated short, mellow whistle.

■**GREATER YELLOWLEGS**   *Tringa melanoleuca*
Long, bright yellow legs. Slender build with long neck. Long, thin
and slightly upturned bill. Brownish gray above; light below. Spotted
except for white belly and rump. Finely barred tail.

Common spring and fall migrant; overwinters in San Juans.
Wades in shallows for small fishes, mussels, and crabs. Call is loud
whistle, repeated 3 to 5 times.

The similar-looking **Lesser Yellowlegs** (*Tringa flavipes*) is smaller
with relatively shorter bill; has softer, 1- to 3-note call. Rare in spring;
more common in fall.

■**RED-NECKED (Northern)
PHALAROPE**   *Phalaropus lobatus*
Swims rather than wades. Very thin, dark bill. Female larger and
more colorful than male. **Winter:** Dark gray above; white below. Dark
line through eye. Broad, white wing stripe. **Summer:** Female has dark
head, white throat; bright red neck and upper breast. Smaller, duller
male has buffy neck and whiter face.

Common in north in fall; uncommon south and in spring. Seen
in flocks on tidal rips and rafts of debris. Feeds on amphipods and
small fishes.

LONG-BILLED DOWITCHER
L 10 in

WHIMBREL
L 14 in

**GREATER
YELLOWLEGS**
L 11 in

Winter

RED-NECKED PHALAROPE
L 6 in

◾ Gulls
Subfamily Larinae
(*Family* Laridae; *Order* Charadriiformes)

Stocky birds with webbed feet; long, pointed wings; and hooked bills. Sexes similar. Juveniles differ visibly from adults; generally darker; adult plumage acquired gradually (2 to 4 years, depending on size of species).

◾ GLAUCOUS-WINGED GULL
Larus glaucescens

Adult: Pale gray wings without black tips. Otherwise white. Pink feet. Yellow bill with red spot. **Juvenile:** Mottled brown with dark bill and legs; grayer second year.

Abundant year-round resident. Scavenges beaches and shallows for fishes, clams, and crabs; drops shellfish onto beach. In summer preys on eggs and young of other seabirds. Familiar gull call.

Herring Gull (*Larus argentatus*) adult is similar but wings have black tips. Uncommon.

Western Gull (*Larus occidentalis*) adult is similar but has uniformly dark brown wings with black tips; large bill. Found mostly on outer coast. Interbreeds with Glaucous-winged.

California Gull (*Larus californicus*) adult is smaller. Has dark gray wings and greenish yellow legs. Common in fall; less common in spring. Breeds in eastern Washington.

◾ THAYER'S GULL
Larus thayeri

Told from Glaucous-winged Gull by dark wing tips, darker feet, and smaller size; from other gulls by pale underside of wing tips.

Common fall through spring in north; less common in south.

◾ HEERMANN'S GULL
Larus heermanni

Our darkest gull. **Adult:** White head with red bill. Dark above; gray below. Black tail edged in white. **Juvenile:** Uniformly dark brown except for thin, white terminal band on tail.

Common in north June to November; less common south. Goes south to breed (southern California). Feeds on schools of Herring and on shrimps; also robs fish from Bonaparte's Gull.

◾ MEW GULL
Larus canus

Adult told by small, yellow, unmarked bill. Yellow legs. Gray wing has white spot on black tip. Otherwise white. Smaller than Glaucous-winged or Thayer's gulls. Upright posture.

Common fall through spring. Picks at insects and small marine creatures on beach, among seaweed, and on water. Call resembles Glaucous-winged Gull's, but higher pitched.

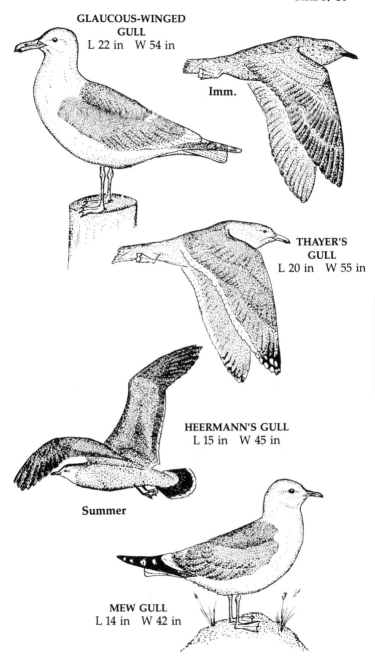

**GLAUCOUS-WINGED
GULL**
L 22 in   W 54 in

Imm.

**THAYER'S
GULL**
L 20 in   W 55 in

HEERMANN'S GULL
L 15 in   W 45 in

Summer

MEW GULL
L 14 in   W 42 in

■**BONAPARTE'S GULL** *Larus philadelphia*
Smallest of our gulls. **Winter:** Adult has gray wing with white tip
edged in black. Otherwise white except for dark smudge behind
black eye. Straight black bill. Orange feet. **Summer:** All-black head.
Bright red feet. **Juvenile:** Resembles winter adult but black band on
tail and diagonal brown lines on wings.

Common spring and fall migrant; some overwinter. Flocks dive,
ternlike, from heights of 3 to 10 feet on small, schooling fishes. Also
picks small creatures from seaweed or beach and hawks insects over
beaches in evening. Call is low quacking.

■**Jaegers** *Subfamily* Stercorariinae (*Family* Laridae)
Predatory seabirds with long, pointed, bent wings. Acrobatic fliers.

■**PARASITIC JAEGER** *Stercorarius parasiticus*
Gull-like body with falconlike, slender, sharply bent wings. Pair of
pointed feathers extends 2 to 4 inches beyond tail. Dark brown
above; light below (usually). Tan band across upper breast. Yellowish wash on upper neck and cheeks (usually). Dark underwings.
Wings and tail edged in black.

Fairly common in fall; rare in spring. Robs terns and Bonaparte's
Gull in acrobatic flight.

■**Terns** *Subfamily* Sterninae (*Family* Laridae)
Buoyant, acrobatic fliers. Dive to take prey.

■**COMMON TERN** *Sterna hirundo*
Slender, pointed gray wings with dark wedge at tip. Long, deeply
forked, white tail; gray outer edge. Flies with bill pointed down.
Summer: Adult has black cap. Red bill with black tip. Red feet. Otherwise white. **Winter** (and juvenile): White forehead.

Fairly common in fall; rare in spring. Dives headfirst from 10 to
30 feet for small fishes and shrimps.

The similar **Arctic Tern** (*Sterna paradisaea*) has all-red bill in summer and gray cheeks. Tips of underwings are lighter. Rare migrant
inshore; but a few breed on Jetty Island near Everett, Washington.

■**CASPIAN TERN** *Sterna caspia*
Largest tern species. Gull-like wide wings and flight; raucous call.
Tail only slightly forked. Black cap. Large red bill. Gray above; white
below.

Uncommon visitor in summer. Often seen near river mouth
deltas. Dives from higher up than other terns; takes larger fish.

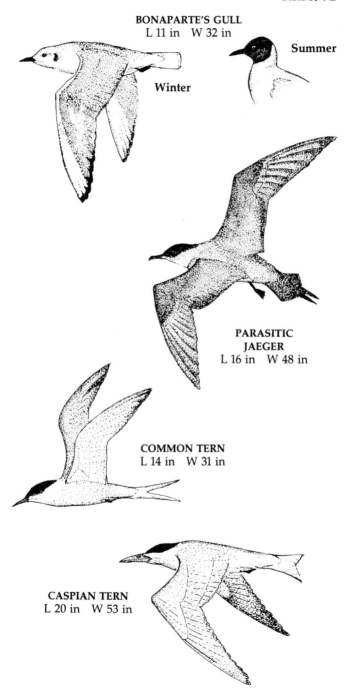

BONAPARTE'S GULL
L 11 in   W 32 in

Winter

Summer

PARASITIC JAEGER
L 16 in   W 48 in

COMMON TERN
L 14 in   W 31 in

CASPIAN TERN
L 20 in   W 53 in

■■■Alcids

Family Alcidae (*Order* Charadriiformes)

Black-and-white seabirds. Come ashore only to breed. Use wings (rather than feet) to swim underwater in the manner of penguins. Sexes similar.

■TUFTED PUFFIN

Fratercula cirrhata

Dark, stubby body. Expanded bill. Orange feet. **Summer:** Adult has yellow and orange-red bill. White face. Long, yellowish tufts from behind eye. Tufts and horny outer bill are shed in fall. Immature is whiter below; smaller, yellow bill.

Seen in summer at eastern end of Strait of Juan de Fuca; nests in excavated tunnels on Protection Island and smaller islets. More common on outer coast. Dives for small fishes, mollusks, and squid; can hold many small Sand Lance or Herring between cornified tongue and roof of mouth.

■COMMON MURRE

Uria aalge

Largest local alcid. Large, dark, spear-shaped bill. Black above, white below. **Winter:** White cheek, throat, and neck. Thin black line curves down from behind eye. **Summer:** All-black head and neck.

Common fall through spring in north; uncommon summer. Breeds on outer coast in late spring and summer. Feeds on small schooling fishes and bottom fishes. Dives to depths of 70 feet to feed on edges of Herring balls.

■PIGEON GUILLEMOT

Cepphus columba

Pigeon shaped. **Summer:** All-black except for white patch with black bars on wing; red feet. **Winter:** Dark above, mottled with white. White wing patch. White below.

Common year-round in north; rare south of Admiralty Inlet in winter. Breeds late spring and summer in rock crevices and in holes in sandy cliffs. Dives for small bottom fishes in shallow water.

TUFTED PUFFIN
L 13 in

Summer

COMMON MURRE
L 14 in

Winter

Summer

PIGEON GUILLEMOT
L 11 in

Summer

Winter

■RHINOCEROS AUKLET   *Cerorhinca monocerata*
Stout, pale yellow bill. Yellow eye. **Winter:** Dark gray above; light
gray breast; white belly and sides. Juvenile has smaller bill and
darker eye. **Summer:** Short "horn" at base of bill. White plumes point
back from above and below eye.

Common spring through fall in north; some overwinter (most
winter at sea). Breeds in excavated tunnels, especially on Protection
Island at eastern end of Strait of Juan de Fuca (17,000 pairs). Dives in
tidal rips to depth of 30 feet for Herring and other small schooling
fishes.

■MARBLED MURRELET   *Brachyramphus marmoratus*
Small and chubby with very short neck. Small, slender bill. **Winter:**
Black above except for white stripe along back; white below. In flight
shows white lines where wings meet back. **Summer:** Dark brown
above; marbled brown below.

Seen year-round, especially at eastern end of Strait of Juan de
Fuca in sheltered water. Nesting locations are still largely unknown.
(The few nests found so far were in old-growth trees or on tundra.)
Dives for small schooling fishes. Pairs call back and forth with high,
stuttering whistle.

The rare **Cassin's Auklet** *(Ptychoramphus aleuticus)* is dark gray
below; has shorter, thicker bill.

■ANCIENT MURRELET   *Synthliboramphus antiquus*
In winter resembles Marbled Murrelet, but bill has pale tip; head is
all-black, contrasting with gray back; lacks white stripe on back.
Winter: Gray above; white below. **Summer:** White, back-pointing
plume above eye. Black-and-white "necklace" behind neck.

Seen fall through spring. Dives, sometimes in synchronized
line, for krill and small fishes. Call is high-pitched squeal.

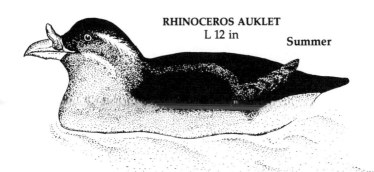

RHINOCEROS AUKLET
L 12 in

Summer

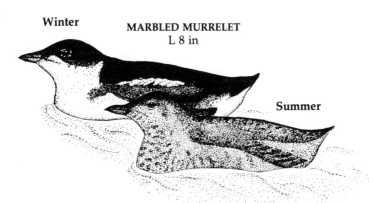

Winter

MARBLED MURRELET
L 8 in

Summer

ANCIENT MURRELET
L 8 in

Winter

■■■ Kingfishers   *Family* Alcedinidae   (*Order* Coraciiformes)

■ BELTED KINGFISHER   *Ceryle alcyon*
Large, crested head. Long, black, spear-shaped bill. Upright perching posture. Deep, irregular wingbeats. Loud, rattling cry. **Male:**
Bluish gray above; white below with gray breast band. **Female:** Similar but with narrow, rusty band on belly.

    Common resident. Seen singly or in pairs perched above water's
edge. Hovers ternlike before plummeting headfirst for small fishes
and crabs. Territorial; noisily chases away rivals, former mates, or
fledged young. Nests in excavated tunnels in sandy cliffs near water.

■■■ Ravens and Crows   *Family* Corvidae
(*Order* Passeriformes)

■ COMMON RAVEN   *Corvus corax*
All-black in all plumages. Resembles crow but is larger; has thicker
bill; shaggy cheeks and throat; shows diamond-shaped tail in flight.
When soaring can be mistaken for hawk.

    Common resident, especially in San Juan and Canadian Gulf is-
lands; rare south of Admiralty Inlet. Nests in remote cliffs and old-
growth forest. Scavenges along beach for carrion. Call is coarse croak.

■ AMERICAN (Common) CROW   *Corvus brachyrhynchos*
Familiar. All-black in all plumages. Unlike Common Raven has
square-cut tail and never soars; smoother neck.

    Commonly seen on intertidal beaches where it scavenges for
crabs, fishes, and carrion. Preys on eggs and chicks in seabird colonies. Call is usually a *caw*, but it sometimes imitates other birds and
beach sounds.

    A smaller race, called the **Northwestern Crow,** is often treated as a
separate species. Found coastally to Alaska. Both local races are
abundant residents with growing populations. Often seen in large
flocks.

♀
**BELTED
KINGFISHER**
L 12 in

COMMON RAVEN
L 21 in   W 50 in

**AMERICAN
CROW**
L 17 in   W 35 in

FISHES

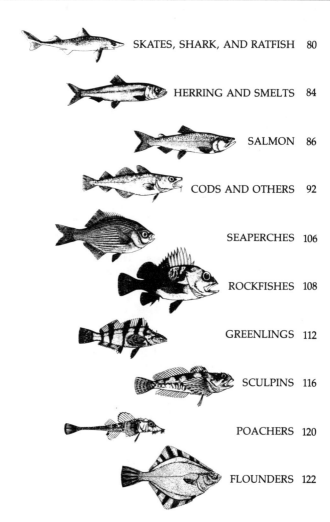

■■■Sharks, Skates, Rays, and Ratfish
Class Chondrichthyes

A broad group of fish families having in common a skeleton of hard cartilage rather than bone. Primitive scales, when present, are rough. Fertilization is internal; eggs are enclosed in tough leather case (purse); males have a copulatory organ (clasper) at each pelvic fin. Cartilaginous fishes evolved before bony fishes, but are still quite varied and successful.

■■Skates
Family Rajidae

Winglike pectoral fins are fused to the snout and flattened front half of body. Rear half of body is taillike with two small dorsal fins set far back; hardly any tail fin. Row of spines often running up tail, sometimes to head. At base of pectoral fin are 2 wide, finlike lateral keels. Internal fertilization. Female deposits small batches of eggs in tough, rectangular cases that often wash up on beaches. Skate species can be distinguished by shape of egg case. (Ratfish and Brown Cat Shark also deposit eggs in cases.)

■BIG SKATE
Raja binoculata

Diamond shape; wider than long. Pointed nose. Spines on tail extend onto body. Dark olive brown to black with numerous light spots. Told from Longnose Skate by lack of long snout and by dark bull's-eye spots at base of winglike pectoral fins. World's largest skate. To over 6 feet.

Found in quiet bays; prefers soft bottoms at moderate depth. Feeds on crustaceans and sculpins and other slow-moving fishes. Leathery, brown, rectangular egg cases; to 1 foot long. Alaska to Mexico.

■LONGNOSE SKATE
Raja rhina

Long, flexible snout. Brown above; bluish below. Dark circles at base of concave pectoral fins. Wide pectoral fins are narrow in front, flare toward back. Pelvic fins are deeply notched. Row of spines along tail rarely extends onto body; 1 or 2 spines on center of head. To over 4 feet.

Caught in same quiet bays as Big Skate. Feeds on worms, clams, sculpins, and other slow-moving fishes. Lays eggs in rectangular, leathery cases; rough with short horns; 3 to 5 inches long. Southeastern Alaska to Baja California.

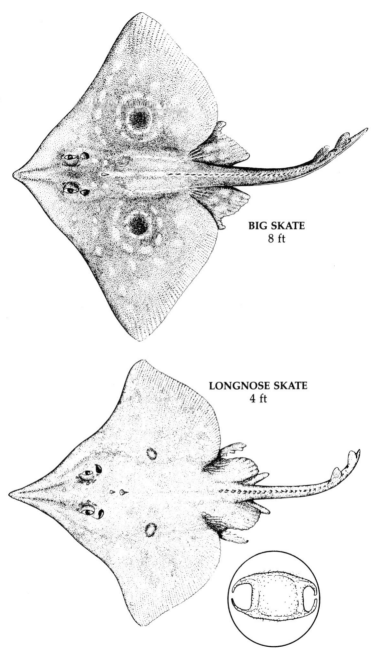

BIG SKATE
8 ft

LONGNOSE SKATE
4 ft

LONGNOSE SKATE EGG CASE
4 in

■ Dogfishes
Family Squalidae

One of 15 families of sharks in the subclass. Sharks have 5 to 7 gill slits on each side. Nine species have been caught locally, but only the Spiny Dogfish is common. The **Brown Cat Shark** (*Apristurus brunneus*) is sometimes caught in deep water in Puget Sound.

■ SPINY DOGFISH
Squalus acanthias

By far the most common local shark. Long, pointed, flattened snout. Two equal-sized dorsal fins, each with sharp spine lying along front edge of fin. No anal fin. Five gill slits before pectoral fin. Adult is brownish gray above, light below; juvenile has 1 or 2 rows of white spots on back. To 5 feet.

Most often seen near the surface at dawn or dusk, or when Herring or salmon are gathered before spawning. Not considered dangerous. Teeth and spines are sharp; should be handled with caution if hooked. Feeds on small crustaceans, Sand Lance, and other small fishes. Alaska to California.

■ Ratfishes
Family Chimaeridae

Live near the bottom, mostly in deep water.

■ SPOTTED RATFISH
Hydrolagus colliei

Distinctive shape. Snout is sharklike with small mouth below. Large, green reflective eyes. Body is stout in front but tapers evenly to long, sharp point in rear. First dorsal fin tall and triangular, preceded by taller, sharp spine (reputedly poisonous). Second dorsal fin divided into 2 long curves. Tail fin and anal fin form a spear-shaped tip. Large pectoral and pelvic fins. Male has club-shaped organ (clasper) on forehead; spiny, club-shaped clasping organs in front of pelvic fins; slender claspers at rear of pelvic fins. Brownish but iridescent with many hues; darker above with lighter, bluish spots. Yellowish fin tips. To about 3 feet.

Sometimes seen in shallow water, especially at night. One of our most abundant fishes at moderate depths. Feeds at night on variety of clams, snails, crabs and other small crustaceans, and small fishes. Southeastern Alaska to Mexico.

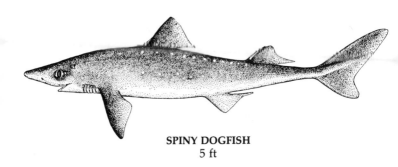

SPINY DOGFISH
5 ft

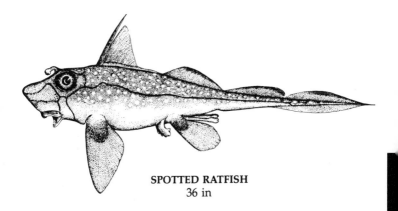

SPOTTED RATFISH
36 in

■■■■ Bony Fishes
Class Osteichthyes

Skeleton of bone, not cartilage. Complex jaw structure. Typical scales.

■■■ Herrings
Family Clupeidae

Includes small schooling fishes: herrings, sardines, and shads.

■ PACIFIC HERRING
Clupea harengus pallasi

Slightly upturned mouth. Silvery color. Lacks distinguishing marks or specialized features. To 12 inches.

Returns from ocean to spawn (February to May) in shallow bays and inlets. Female deposits adhesive eggs on Eelgrass or seaweed in shallow water. Larva hatches 2 weeks later; dispersed by tidal currents. Vulnerable to oil and surface chemicals during this period. Juvenile seen in large schools in shallow water in summer.

Adults form large tight schools (Herring balls); feed on shrimps and small fishes; juvenile feeds on plankton. Very important prey species for salmon and other large fishes, diving birds, and Minke Whale. Important baitfish. Formerly harvested from canoes with "herring rakes" by Indians (also collected eggs on submerged evergreen boughs). Japan to northern Alaska to Baja California.

■■■ Smelts
Family Osmeridae

Small, slender fishes with salmonlike adipose fins. Most school in deep water; return to beaches or rivers to spawn.

■ SURF SMELT
Hypomesus pretiosus

Small mouth. Forked tail. Bright, horizontal reflecting line along side (turns dark when fish is dead). Light brownish green above; silvery, iridescent below. To 8 inches.

Adult common in open water; juvenile in shallows (sometimes enters rivers). Spawns May to February. Sticky eggs deposited on intertidal gravel just before high tide. Larva goes directly into plankton; feeds on progressively larger plankton as it grows. Adult feeds on isopods, copepods, and other small crustaceans; preyed on by salmon and other large fishes. Formerly caught by Indians with herring rakes; now netted from piers. A commercial delicacy fish in British Columbia. Central Alaska to southern California.

■ EULACHON (Candlefish)
Thaleichthys pacificus

Told from other smelts by relatively long anal fin. Bluish or brownish above; silvery sides and belly. Striations on gill cover. To 10 inches.

Anadromous; returns in large numbers in spring to spawn in large rivers. Feeds on planktonic crustaceans. Spawning runs preyed on by large fishes, sea lions, Orca, diving birds, and gulls. Fished commercially on Fraser River; sold as a delicacy. So oily it was used as candle. Was important source of Indian dietary and lamp oil; rendered oil distributed inland over so-called grease trails. Central Alaska to central California.

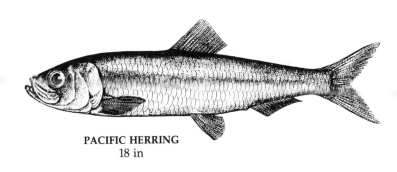

PACIFIC HERRING
18 in

SURF SMELT
12 in

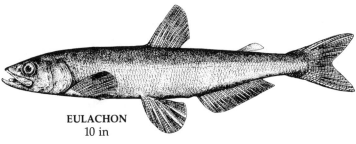

EULACHON
10 in

■ Salmon, Trouts, and Chars

Family Salmonidae

Medium-to-large, torpedo-shaped fish. Powerful swimmers. Small dorsal adipose fin (between dorsal fin and tail) separates the family from all but the smaller, slenderer smelts.

Most salmonids are anadromous, spending adult life in salt water and returning to breed in freshwater streams. Breeding adults undergo radical changes in color when entering fresh water; males develop a hooked jaw, large canine teeth, and "razor back."

Spawning females dig redds (shallow nests) in bottom gravels; lay small, round eggs that males fertilize with milt (sperm); and cover eggs with gravel. Pacific salmon die soon after mating, but some sea-run trout breed 2 or 3 times. Eggs spend 2 to 5 months in stream-bed gravel. Need clear, well-oxygenated water; many smothered by sediments eroded from logging roads, logged stream banks, and streamside construction.

Pink and Chum fry migrate downstream right after hatching. Chinook, Coho, and Steelhead stay in streams 6 months to 2 years. Sockeye fry moves to lakes to feed on freshwater plankton for first 1 to 2 years. Juvenile salmon need estuaries for transition to salt water and for early growth.

Hydroelectric and irrigation dams now block off thousands of miles of salmonid breeding streams. Dams kill smolts as they migrate to the sea. As mitigation, dozens of hatcheries have been built with public funds, but effectiveness (and adverse genetic effects) of the hatchery programs are controversial.

■ CHINOOK (King) SALMON

Oncorhynchus tshawytscha

Black gums. Small black spots on dark back and both lobes of tail; silver sides. Called king or tyee when mature, blackmouth when immature. Largest salmon; locally to 70 pounds (15 to 20 pounds average).

Most diverse life history of any Pacific salmonid. Spring-run population breeds February to April; prefers to spawn on large gravel in deep riffles in headwaters of glacial rivers and larger tributaries. Fall-run populations return to rivers July to November (peak late August); tend to spawn in lower reaches of main stems of rivers.

Fingerlings feed on stream insects. Fall-run smolts migrate downstream during first spring; spring-run stay in stream for full year. Juveniles gain weight in estuary for 1 to 3 months, then move to deeper water. Eat planktonic animals at first, then small fishes.

Adult spends 3 to 5 years in salt water, traveling north along coastal British Columbia and around the Gulf of Alaska. Male matures at 2 to 5 years; female at 4 to 5 years. Some precocious males (jacks) return early to breed, but large kings are more than 5 years old. Breeding male has strongly hooked jaw. See at Lake Washington Ship Canal fish ladder (peaks late August). Japan to Alaska to southern California.

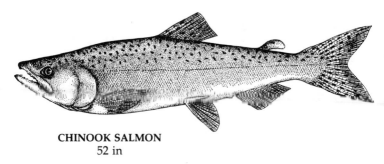

CHINOOK SALMON
52 in

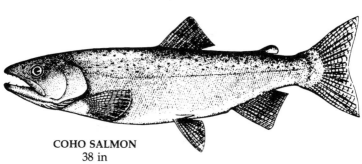

COHO SALMON
38 in

■**COHO (Silver) SALMON**   *Oncorhynchus kisutch*
White gums. No spots on lower tail. In salt water has bluish back and
silvery sides; small round spots on back and upper lobe of tail.
Breeding male has green head and back, bright red sides. Female is
paler. Smaller and slimmer than Chinook: averages 30 inches, 6 to 12
pounds (to 38 inches, 30 pounds). Prefers open water; nearer surface
than Chinook.

Seen year-round but peaks during fall migration (August to November). Enters streams September to October. Spawns October to
December; prefers gravel in small, unspoiled streams.

Fry is aggressive and territorial; stays in stream for over a year,
feeding on aquatic insect larvae, drift insects, and small fishes; smolt
is relatively large when reaching estuary the following spring. Juvenile stays week to month in estuary, schooling over cobble beach and
feeding on small crustaceans. Eventually moves to open water where
it feeds on large plankton and larval fishes; graduates to larger fishes
as it grows.

At sea feeds on Herring, Sand Lance, squids, and amphipods.
Returns to breed at 3 years old (2-year-old jacks are common in
hatchery runs). Next to Sockeye in commercial value; prized as sport
fish. See at Lake Washington Ship Canal fish ladder (peaks late September). Japan to Alaska to Baja California.

■SOCKEYE (Red) SALMON   *Oncorhynchus nerka*

Small pupils (⅓ size of eye). Lacks distinct spots. Greenish blue back is speckled; sides silvery. Breeding adult has bright scarlet body and fins; pale green head. Adult averages 5 to 7 pounds (to 33 inches, 15 pounds).

Spends 2 to 3 years at sea; moves rapidly through Strait of Juan de Fuca June to October. Spawns in tributary to lake or in lakeshore. After hatching, fry moves quickly to lake. Spends 1 or 2 years in lake in tight schools, feeding on freshwater plankton. Large smolt migrates to estuary April to June; feeds on euphausiids, juvenile shrimp, and crab larvae. Quickly leaves estuary for high seas rearing grounds; found far out along Aleutian Islands.

Introduced to Lake Washington in the 1930s. See at Lake Washington Ship Canal fish ladder (peaks July). Japan to Alaska to southern California (rare south of Columbia River).

■CHUM (Dog) SALMON   *Oncorhynchus keta*

Large pupils (½ eye diameter). Back and sides speckled, but lack black spots. Paired fins dark tipped. Breeding adult dark olive green with red and brown splotchy vertical bars on sides. Averages 25 inches, 9 pounds (to 40 inches, 33 pounds).

After 3 to 5 years at sea returns in several runs (late fall to early winter). Moves quickly through inland waters to spawn in lower reaches of small coastal streams. After emerging from gravel, fry immediately migrates to salt water. Spends month or more in estuary in dense schools; likes Eelgrass beds; feeds on Harpacticoid Copepods.

At 2-inch size, juvenile moves to open surface waters; eats variety of planktonic crustaceans. Preyed on by adult Cutthroat and Dolly Varden. Moves to sea in fall; swims north along coast and out along Aleutian Islands. Japan to Alaska to southern California.

■PINK (Humpback) SALMON   *Oncorhynchus gorbuscha*

Large, oval dark spots on back and on both lobes of tail fin. Metallic blue back, silver sides. Breeding male develops large hump on olive green back; green blends into red on sides. Breeding female has olive sides with brown blotches. Adult averages 4 to 6 pounds (to 30 inches, 12 pounds).

Adult returns to spawn after 2 years at sea (the shortest salmon maturity). Returns to Puget Sound and Fraser River in odd-numbered years. Enters streams September to November; immediately spawns in small streams and tributaries close to sea.

Eggs hatch February to May. Fry migrates to sea soon after emergence. Spends month or two in estuaries, initially in Eelgrass beds, marshes, and beaches. Feeds on zooplankton. Preyed on by adult Cutthroat and Dolly Varden. Swims in tight schools along shallows. Moves north up coast of British Columbia and Alaska; circles back not far offshore. Japan to Alaska to California.

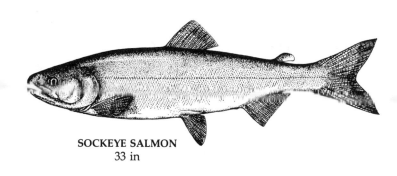

SOCKEYE SALMON
33 in

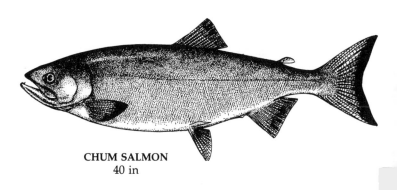

CHUM SALMON
40 in

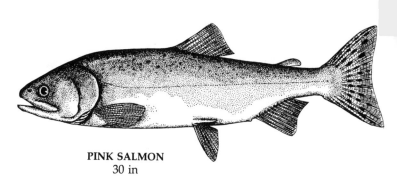

PINK SALMON
30 in

■RAINBOW (Steelhead) TROUT   *Salmo gairdneri*

Large, seagoing rainbow trout; more closely related to Atlantic salmon than to Pacific species. Greenish back and silvery sides; black spots on back, sides, tail, and dorsal fin. Head is relatively short. Breeding male has red on cheeks and along sides; jaw elongates at each return to fresh water. Adult averages 5 to 20 pounds depending on number of breeding cycles (to 45 inches, 43 pounds.)

Adult returns to spawn in 2 separate runs. Summer-run adult arrives fall to winter, storing fat before heading upstream the following April to September. Winter-run adult arrives 1 to 2 months before ascending streams November to March. Since many individuals breed repeatedly, they are also caught on return trip to sea.

Young spends 2 to 3 years in streams, feeding on stream insects. Migrating smolt feeds on crab larvae, insects, and small crustaceans. Wide-ranging adult spends marine phase far out at sea. A favorite sport fish in rivers. See at Lake Washington Ship Canal fish ladder (peaks January). Japan to Alaska to Baja California.

■CUTTHROAT TROUT   *Salmo clarki clarki*

Black spots over entire body (except paired fins). Greenish blue back shades to silver sides. Red "cutthroat marks" beneath jaw faint at sea but darken as breeding adult moves upstream. Sea-run adult reaches 10 to 24 inches, 2 to 4 pounds. Nonmigratory ones are larger (to 20 pounds).

Seen year-round; usually in shallow water close to shore. Prefers estuarine conditions, where it feeds on amphipods, isopods, shrimps, and young fishes, including Pink and Chum salmon.

Ascends rivers late summer through fall; spawns late winter to early spring. Most spawn twice; a few 3 or more times. Some fry go immediately to sea; others stay in stream indefinitely. Japan to Alaska to central California.

■DOLLY VARDEN   *Salvelinus malma*

Dark silver to blue or green; lighter below. Pale yellow or red spots on sides. Leading edges of pelvic and anal fins cream colored. Reach 5 pounds (to 36 inches, 30 pounds). Landlocked ones larger.

Found year-round in estuaries, near river mouths and along shore. Mature (4 to 5 years) adult ascends streams July to January (peaks October to November) after 2 years in salt water. Spawns slightly earlier than Steelhead. Fry stays 1 to 3 years in rivers; migrates to estuary (often with Steelhead) April to May. Korea to Alaska to Oregon.

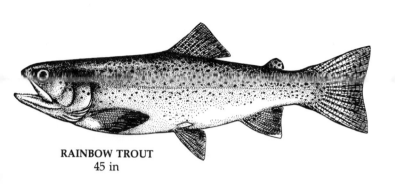

RAINBOW TROUT
45 in

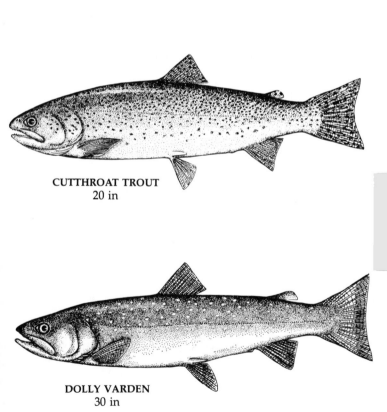

CUTTHROAT TROUT
20 in

DOLLY VARDEN
30 in

■ Codfishes
Family Gadidae

Includes true cods, tomcods, and pollocks. Most species have 3 separate dorsal fins; rear 2 matched by 2 anal fins.

Adults usually found in deep water; often move into shallower water in spring and summer. Juveniles found near shore. Important commercial fishes.

■ PACIFIC COD
Gadus macrocephalus

Three separate dorsal fins; 2 separate anal fins. Long barbel hangs from lower lip. First dorsal fin rounded. Mottled brownish gray above; lighter below. Dusky fins, often white edged. To 45 inches.

Common near bottom in deep water; sometimes found in shallow water in summer. Feeds on worms, crabs, clams, shrimps, and smaller fishes. Important commercial fish; caught by trawlers for frozen fillets. Adults concentrate during winter spawning and are caught recreationally. Japan to California.

Similar-looking **Walleye (Pacific) Pollock** (Theragra chalcogramma) lacks barbel. Sharply triangular first dorsal fin. Lower jaw extends slightly past upper. Juvenile is common in schools near shore over sand or mud bottom. Adult (to 3 feet) is commercially important.

Pacific Hake (Merluccius productus) has only 2 dorsal fins, 1 anal fin. Abundant in bottom trawls; washes up on beaches. Important prey for California Sea Lion.

■ PACIFIC TOMCOD
Microgadus proximus

Small chin barbel (length of eye pupil). First dorsal fin is shark shaped. **Adult:** Mottled brown-olive above; creamy below. Fins dusky tipped. Gill covers have purple iridescence. **Juvenile:** Translucent fins. To 12 inches.

Common from surface to deep water. Schooling juveniles seen over sandy bottoms at night. Juvenile feeds on zooplankton such as copepods; adults on larger crustaceans such as shrimp. Little studied. Bering Sea to central California.

■ Sablefishes
Family Anoplopomatidae

Only 2 species in family. More closely related to rockfishes and sculpins than to cods, despite common name of local species.

■ SABLEFISH (Blackcod)
Anoplopoma fimbria

Sleek, torpedo body. Two well-separated, nearly equal dorsal fins; first has more than 15 spines. First dorsal fin edged with black; edges of other fins pale. Forked tail. Back is bluish or greenish black to gray; silver below. At sea can reach 40 inches, 125 pounds. Young caught in shallow local waters in summer are about 2 to 3 years old, weigh about 2 pounds.

Common inland when young; moves to sea when older and during winter. Feeds on small crustaceans, worms, and small fishes. Fished commercially off Alaska and British Columbia. Oily; good for smoking. Japan to Alaska to Baja California.

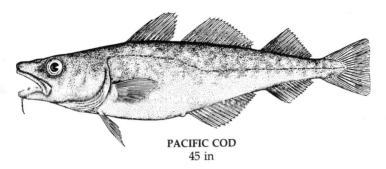

PACIFIC COD
45 in

PACIFIC HAKE
36 in

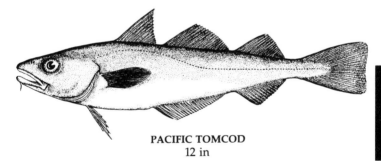

PACIFIC TOMCOD
12 in

SABLEFISH
40 in

■Toadfishes

Family Batrachoididae

■PLAINFIN MIDSHIPMAN

Porichthys notatus

Rows of photophores (luminous organs) along lower sides and undersides. Large mouth; small eye. White cheeks. Tapering body. Lacks scales. Dorsal and anal fins are long and even. Iridescent brown, green, or purple above; golden below. To 15 inches.

Common from intertidal to deep water. Nocturnal; often buries itself in sand during day. Adult has about 700 photophores. Ours does not luminesce, perhaps because it lacks Ostracode prey, which supplies needed chemical. Known to emit loud grunts and croaks. Migrates offshore in winter; in spring and summer moves into shallows to spawn. Female lays egg mass under rock; male guards and fans eggs of many females. Southeastern Alaska to Baja California

■Sand Lances

Family Ammodytidae

Small family of schooling fishes that bury themselves in sand.

■PACIFIC SAND LANCE
(Sand Eel; Candlefish)

Ammodytes hexapterus

Slender, almost cylindrical body. Long, even dorsal fin. Long, sharp lower jaw. Iridescent gray or greenish above; silvery below. To 8 inches.

Common in large dense schools in shallows over clean sand. Lacks the air-filled swim bladder most fish possess and so must swim to keep position. Often rests on sand during day; burrows into sand at night or if disturbed. Larva eats phytoplankton and is preyed on by Herring. Juvenile eats zooplankton. Adult feeds on variety of small organisms; preyed on by salmon and many other large fishes, and by Minke Whales and other marine mammals. Japan to Alaska to southern California.

■Wolffishes

Family Anarhichadidae

Other wolffishes are large but stubby and live in the north Atlantic. The Wolf-eel differs in body shape but has similar habits.

■WOLF-EEL

Anarrhichthys ocellatus

Robust head; small eyes. Long, tapering body (often confused with moray eel, which is not found locally). Wrinkled face with large teeth. Male has larger head, thicker lips. Dorsal and ventral fins low and long; meet at pointed rear of body. No tail fin, pelvic fin, or lateral line. Color variable: gray-blue, orange, brown, or green; large darker spots over body and dorsal fin. To 8 feet.

Fairly common, but inconspicuous; from shallow to moderate depths. Fierce looking but harmless. Leads secluded life in rocky cave or crevice. Uses powerful jaws to crush clams, sea urchins, crabs, and fishes. Pairs may live together and breed over successive seasons. One or both parents guard egg mass. Japan to Alaska to southern California.

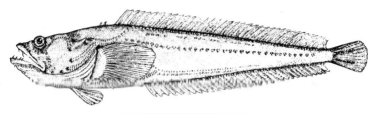

PLAINFIN MIDSHIPMAN
15 in

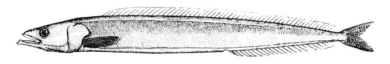

PACIFIC SAND LANCE
8 in

WOLF-EEL
8 ft

■ Sticklebacks
Family Gasterosteidae

■ THREESPINE STICKLEBACK
Gasterosteus aculeatus

Spinous front half of dorsal fin reduced to 3 sharp spines (2 large and 1 small) in front of soft-rayed posterior dorsal fin; front spines lock up when fish is threatened. Slender, keeled caudal peduncle (stem of tail). Bony plates along side. Translucent fins. Silvery green to in-ｈ ……ｏ ｌｉｌｎｉ ｉｌｉ ｌｉｌｉ ｈ Ｔｉ ｄ ｌｉｉ ｌｉ ｓ

Abundant in sheltered estuarine bays in Eelgrass or near pilings. Swims, in part, by waving pectoral fins. Feeds on copepods, other small crustaceans, and fish larvae. Preyed on by larger fishes, seals, and seabirds.

Two distinct phases: some populations live entirely in fresh water; others live in salt water but return to river mouths to breed. Breeding male is fiercely territorial; engages in elaborate courtship displays; builds and defends nests of algae. Found throughout Northern Hemisphere.

■ TUBE-SNOUT
Aulorhynchus flavidus

Very slender body. Long, narrow snout with tiny mouth. First half of dorsal fin reduced to small spines along back; second portion triangular (similar to and above anal fin). Mottled tan or olive above; creamy below. Dark line between eye and front of pectoral fin; silvery patch below. Told from Bay Pipefish by stouter body, paired dorsal and anal fins, and larger tail fin. To 7 inches.

Abundant in sheltered bays in Eelgrass or kelp beds. Sometimes seen in large schools, usually in shallow water. Swims with jerky motion. Feeds on planktonic copepods and fish larvae. Breeding male defends nest built of seaweed connected with strands of adhesive extruded from genital region. Central Alaska to northern Baja California.

■ Pipefishes and Seahorses
Family Syngnathidae

■ BAY PIPEFISH
Syngnathus leptorhynchus

Extremely slender, flexible body. Covered by bony plates. Lacks fins. Minute mouth; tiny tail fin. Shades of brown or green, depending on environment. Translucent fins. Told from Tube-snout by even more slender body; rectangular dorsal fin; lack of pelvic fin; and tiny tail fin. To 13 inches.

Common in Eelgrass beds and around wharves in shallow water. Swims slowly, jerkily, often vertically by undulating dorsal fin and flicking pectoral fins. Sucks copepods, amphipods, and crab larvae into tubular mouth. In summer male incubates eggs in brood pouch on abdomen. Central Alaska to Baja California.

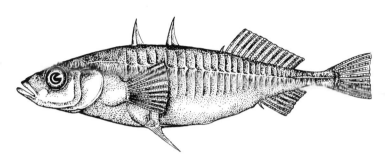

THREESPINE STICKLEBACK
4 in

TUBE-SNOUT
7 in

BAY PIPEFISH
13 in

98/FISHES

■Gunnels
Family Pholididae

Slender, compressed, eellike bodies. Low, soft dorsal fin extends length of body. Anal fin also reaches tail fin; just half as long. Found in shallow rocky areas and tide pools. Spawn in winter at lower levels of rocky intertidal beaches. Not well-known despite abundance.

■PENPOINT GUNNEL
Apodichthys flavidus

"Penpoint" spine under skin at forward edge of anal fin. Diagonal black line leading back and down from eye. Color varies with environment and diet: mostly bright green, sometimes red, yellow, or brown. Line of dark dots along middle of sides. To 18 inches.

A "blenny eel" found wriggling under rocks and seaweed on intertidal beaches. Very common, but not well-known. Feeds on amphipods, copepods, mysids, and isopods. Male (or perhaps both parents) wraps around eggs. Gulf of Alaska to southern California.

■CRESCENT GUNNEL
Pholis laeta

Row of bright white or gold spots enclosed by opposing crescent-shaped markings ("parentheses") along top of back. Thick, dark vertical or diagonal line (often) passes through eye. Mottled lime color; darker above, lighter below. To 10 inches.

Another "blenny eel" found wriggling under rocks and seaweed on intertidal beaches; also subtidal to moderate depths. Feeds on amphipods and other small crustaceans. Parent wraps around eggs. Bering Sea to northern California.

■SADDLEBACK GUNNEL
Pholis ornata

Series of U- or V-shaped black markings along upper back extending onto dorsal fin. Sometimes line or lines through eye. Olive to brown above; dark, irregular vertical bars on lower sides; yellow to red below. To 12 inches.

Another "blenny eel" found wriggling under intertidal rocks. Feeds on small crustaceans such as amphipods and mysids. Central British Columbia to central California.

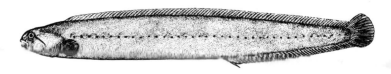

PENPOINT GUNNEL
18 in

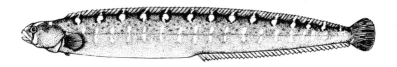

CRESCENT GUNNEL
10 in

SADDLEBACK GUNNEL
12 in

■ **Pricklebacks** *Family* Stichaeidae

Small bottom dwellers with long, laterally compressed bodies similar to gunnels. Low dorsal fin extends from head to tail; similar anal fin extends from midbody to tail. Dorsal fin is "prickly"; many species have cirri or fleshy crests (some bizarre) on head region.

■ **HIGH COCKSCOMB** *Anoplarchus purpurescens*

Fleshy crest on top of head. Head and eyes proportionately larger than similar-looking gunnels. Color extremely variable: shades of olive, brown, purple, or black. Back is darkest; dorsal fin often shows dark vertical stripes. Gray bar at base of striped tail fin. No pelvic fins. Female slightly larger; more subdued coloration and more mottled. Breeding male's dorsal and tail fins turn red; other fins turn orange. To over 7 inches.

Most common "blenny eel" in north. Found wriggling under intertidal rocks and in tide pools; often in groups of 6 or more. Feeds on amphipods, worms, and small clams. Breeding male becomes territorial. Female coils around egg masses. Bering Sea to southern California.

■ **MOSSHEAD WARBONNET** *Chirolophis nugator*

Mossy growth of even-sized cirri covers head. **Female:** Brown. **Male:** Shades of brown tinged with red; mottled with pale bars on sides. Series of 12 or so dark spots in clear circles along dorsal fin. To 5 inches.

Uncommon. Hides in cracks and holes on rocky beaches and subtidally. Life history not well-known. Aleutian Islands to southern California.

■ **SNAKE PRICKLEBACK** *Lumpenus sagitta*

Very elongated body. Dark bars on tail. Rounded head with small, straight mouth. Light green shading to white on underside; dark streaks on side. To 20 inches.

Common on sandy or muddy bottom and Eelgrass beds. Rests on pectoral and pelvic fins. Juvenile is abundant near surface off river mouths in spring; feeds on copepods. Adult feeds on small clams, crustaceans, and worms. Japan to Alaska to northern California.

■ **ROCK PRICKLEBACK** *Xiphister mucosus*

Very low dorsal fin. Small tail fin. Two or 3 pale bands edged with black diverge from eyes. (Similar **Black Prickleback** [*Xiphister atropupureus*] has 3 dark bands edged with white. Common in north.) Greenish black with several dusky white bars near rear of sides. To 20 inches.

Another "blenny eel" found wriggling in tide pools or under intertidal rocks covered with green algae, on which it feeds. Southeastern Alaska to southern California.

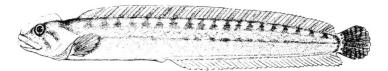

HIGH COCKSCOMB
7 in

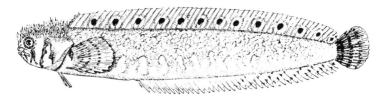

MOSSHEAD WARBONNET
5 in

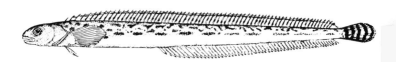

SNAKE PRICKLEBACK
20 in

ROCK PRICKLEBACK
20 in

■Clingfishes
Family Gobiesocidae

Large adhesive disk on breast is formed by the uniting of modified pelvic fins. Not closely related to similar-looking snailfishes. No scales.

■NORTHERN CLINGFISH
Gobiesox maeandricus

Large adhesive disk beneath body. Tadpole shape from above or below. Head large and compressed. Dorsal fin set back on body above anal fin. Olive green to cherry red; mottled with reticulated pattern of lighter shades. To 6 inches.

Common in tide pools or rocky areas; clings to undersides of rocks or to kelp. Feeds on limpets and other mollusks, amphipods, isopods, and mysids. In late winter to early spring female attaches concentric rings of yellow eggs to undersides of rock. Male guards egg mass. Southeastern Alaska to southern California.

■Snailfishes and Lumpfishes
Family Cyclopteridae

Small to medium size. Most have pelvic fins modified as disk; adhere to underside of rocks. Not closely related to similar-looking clingfishes.

■SHOWY SNAILFISH
Liparis pulchellus

Tadpole shape. Broad head with widely spaced eyes. Told from other snailfishes by miniscule tail fin (other species have distinct tail fin); long dorsal and anal fins join. Brown above; tan below. Wavy, horizontal, red lines or spots on sides. To 10 inches.

The most common snailfish in Puget Sound; less so farther north. Soviet Union to Alaska to central California.

■PACIFIC SPINY LUMPSUCKER
Eumicrotremus orbis

Odd roundish shape. Large eye. **Female:** Pale green. Covered with large tubercles. **Male:** Dull orange to reddish brown. Smaller tubercles. To 5 inches.

Common around San Juan and Canadian Gulf islands where current is swift over rocky bottoms; uncommon in inner Puget Sound. Slow swimmer; swims backward and forward. Soviet Union to Alaska to Puget Sound.

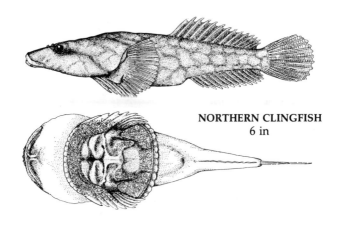

NORTHERN CLINGFISH
6 in

SHOWY SNAILFISH
10 in

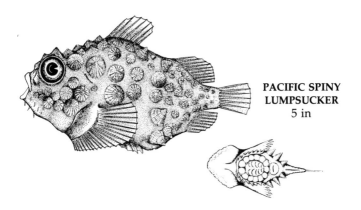

**PACIFIC SPINY
LUMPSUCKER**
5 in

■ Gobies

Family Gobiidae

Small, active bottom dwellers; dart around, then rest on fins. Often burrow in mud or live in burrows of other organisms.

■ BLACKEYE GOBY

Coryphopterus nicholsi

Large eyes; black pupils. Fused, enlarged pelvic fins used for resting, not suction. Round tail fin. Fleshy crest on top of head. Large body scales. Third spine of first dorsal fin. Dorsal and anal fins paired. Pectoral fins translucent. Orange to olive with faint streaks of purplish brown, flecked with metallic green. Iridescent blue spots under eyes. Bluish trailing edge of tail and anal fin. During breeding season male pelvic fin turns black; other colors become more brilliant. Male to 5 inches; female slightly smaller.

Common in quiet, shallow to moderately deep water over rocky reefs or rocks on sand. Conspicuously exposed and territorial, especially male during breeding season. Male digs nest beneath rock; guards eggs from predators. Feeds on copepods and amphipods. Northern British Columbia to Baja California.

■ BAY GOBY

Lepidogobius lepidus

Fused pelvic fins form hollow cone on stalk. Also told from Blackeye Goby by thinner body, smaller eyes, smaller scales, striped, oval tail fin, and wider gap between dorsal fins. Pale olive green; mottled with darker patches on back. Tail and second dorsal fin lightly striped. To 4 inches.

Common in intertidal to moderately deep water over muddy bottoms. Northern British Columbia to Baja California.

Arrow Goby (*Clevelandia ios*) is similar but much smaller (to 2 inches); lacks dark tips of first dorsal fin; mouth extends behind eye. Pale gray, green, or tawny; fine speckling. Dark bars or spotting on fins. In spring belly turns yellow (brighter on female); black streaks appear on the anal fins. Can be found over muddy beaches; lives in burrows of Mud Shrimp or Ghost Shrimp. Central British Columbia to Baja California.

■ Eelpouts

Family Zoarcidae

■ BLACKBELLY EELPOUT

Lycodopsis pacifica

Large head with short upper jaw. Slender tapering body. Long, even dorsal and anal fins, which join at tail. Lacks tail fin. Pale gray to brown above; black shows through on belly. Black spots on front of dorsal fin. To 18 inches.

Common over muddy bottoms at moderate depths. Most common of 5 similar-looking local eelpout species. Feeds on clams, polychaete worms, and small crabs. Central Alaska to southern California.

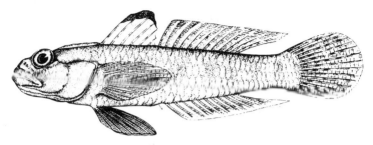

BLACKEYE GOBY
5 in

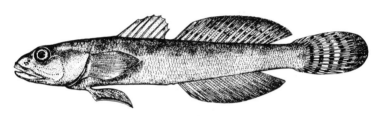

BAY GOBY
4 in

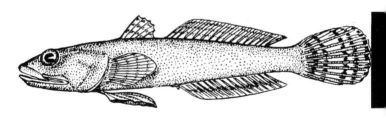

ARROW GOBY
2 in

**BLACKBELLY
EELPOUT**
18 in

■ Seaperches (Surfperches) *Family* Embiotocidae

Oval, highly compressed bodies. Forked tails. Swim with rowing motion of pectoral fins. Found in shallow water near rocks or pilings with kelp; move to deeper water in winter. Give live birth to up to 40 well-developed young.

■ SHINER PERCH *Cymatogaster aggregata*

Silvery sides, horizontal black stripes broken by 3 vertical yellow bars. (Breeding male turns dark, obscuring bars.) Greenish back. Unpaired fins translucent. To 6 inches.

Abundant in shallow water in summer; moves deeper in winter. Seen in schools in bays and estuaries, especially Eelgrass beds. Well developed at birth; male can breed after just a few months. Adult feeds on mussels, small crustaceans, worms, and snails. Southeastern Alaska to Baja California.

■ STRIPED SEAPERCH *Embiotoca lateralis*

About 15 horizontal blue stripes on dark copper or reddish background. Bright blue streaks on head. Juvenile is bright golden. Spiny front half of dorsal fin is short; soft rear half is taller and darker. To 15 inches.

Abundant (in schools) along kelp-covered rocky shores, near pilings, and in Eelgrass beds. Feeds on amphipods, barnacles, mussels, worms, and Herring eggs. Southeastern Alaska to Baja California.

■ PILE PERCH *Rhacochilus vacca*

Dusky vertical bar down center of silver-gray side. Dark gray back; silver belly. Front half of dorsal fin low, progressively taller; rear half tall in front, then curves lower. Deeply forked tail fin. To 17 inches.

Abundant (singly or in small schools) along rocky shores, pilings, and kelp beds; also seen near surface in kelp fronds. Feeds mostly on isopods, amphipods, mussels, and small crabs; pharyngeal teeth adapted to crushing shells. Fished off docks. Southeastern Alaska to Baja California.

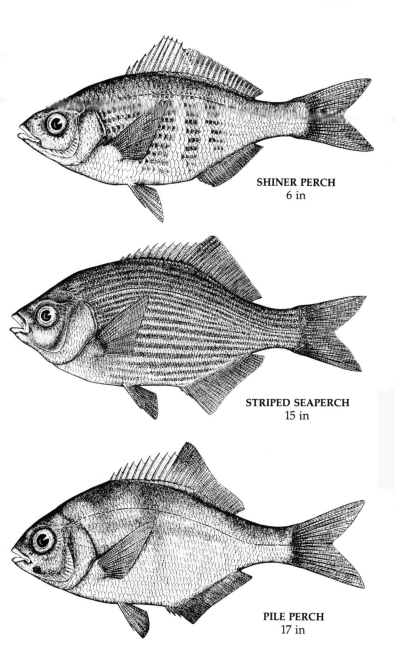

SHINER PERCH
6 in

STRIPED SEAPERCH
15 in

PILE PERCH
17 in

■ Rockfishes
Family Scorpaenidae

Medium size, slow moving; usually found near rocks. Large head, eyes, and mouth; well-developed spiny fins that are mildly poisonous. Large dorsal fin divided into spiny front section and softer rear section. Shallow-water species are typically brownish or greenish; deep-water species reddish. Adults give birth to live young in large broods. All but 1 of our 26 species are in genus *Sebastes*.

■ COPPER ROCKFISH
Sebastes caurinus

Concave forehead (top of eyes level with it). Lower jaw barely extends past upper. Back is coppery with white, pink, or yellow blotches. Often pale stripe along rear of lateral line. Whitish undersides extend up lower sides. Dark on dorsal fin; fins otherwise light. Grows to 20 inches, 10 pounds.

Solitary. Most abundant local rockfish in shallow water. Found near reefs and rock piles. Feeds on small crustaceans and fishes. A favorite sport fish. Gulf of Alaska to Baja California.

■ BROWN ROCKFISH
Sebastes auriculatus

Tan mottled with darker brown across back and head. Dark blotch on gill cover. Flat bare space between eyes. Dusky pink or yellow on fins and lower part of head. Lower jaw barely longer than upper. Pinkish belly and lower fins. To 20 inches.

Relatively common in Puget Sound, less so in straits of Juan de Fuca and Georgia. Prefers kelp beds at shallow to moderate depths. Gives birth to live young in June. Southeastern Alaska to Baja California.

■ BLACK ROCKFISH
Sebastes melanops

Smooth, curved forehead. Large mouth with weak knob on end of chin. Rear half of dorsal fin taller than spinous front half. Tail fin squared off. Back is bluish black; sides are gray with black spots; belly light. Dark fins. To 23 inches.

Common around rocky points or rock walls or in kelp beds in shallow to moderately deep water; often in schools at the surface. Some populations may migrate offshore to spawn. Young born in spring. Feeds on amphipods and small fishes. Taken by divers, commercial and sport fishermen. Aleutian Islands to southern California.

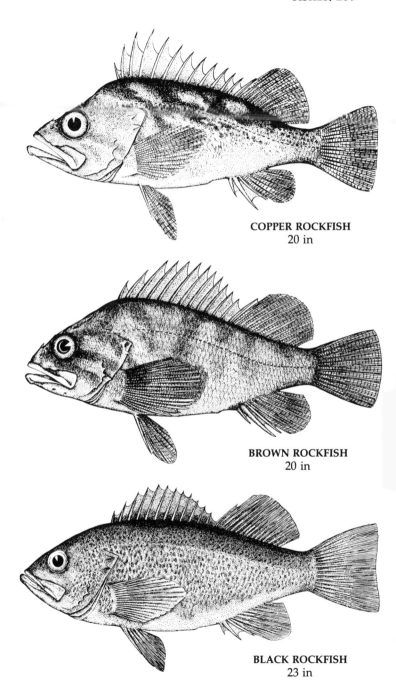

COPPER ROCKFISH
20 in

BROWN ROCKFISH
20 in

BLACK ROCKFISH
23 in

■**YELLOWTAIL ROCKFISH**   *Sebastes flavidus*
Smooth, straight forehead. Lower jaw extends well past the upper.
Knob on chin. Tail fin slightly concave. Rear edge of the anal fin is
vertical. Rather uniform brown or olive, sometimes speckled with
red; pale splotches on back below dorsal fin. Fin tips are yellow or
greenish. To 26 inches.

Common in Puget Sound and Strait of Georgia. While more
common offshore than near shore; juveniles seen near piers. Found
in schools, from surface to deep water. Feeds on small planktonic
crustaceans and fishes. Fished commercially by trawlers or long-
liners. Gulf of Alaska to southern California.

■**PUGET SOUND ROCKFISH**   *Sebastes emphaeus*
Small; often mistaken for juvenile of other rockfishes. Dorsal fin
weakly indented. Slender body; reddish gold with brown or greenish
blotches and dark horizontal stripe below lateral line. To 6 inches.

Found singly or in loose schools above rocky bottoms. Seen by
divers, but caught only incidently by anglers. Feeds on copepods,
jellyfishes, crab larvae, and other small planktonic animals. Gulf of
Alaska to northern California.

■**QUILLBACK ROCKFISH**   *Sebastes maliger*
Tall, spinous dorsal fin, deeply incised at anterior. Posterior dark
brown to black; anterior orange (with some dark spotting), including
front of dorsal fin. Large light blotch over gill cover. No stripe along
lateral line. To 22 inches.

Common and widely distributed throughout the inland waters.
Solitary bottom dweller near rocks in shallow water. A favorite sport
fish of divers; fished commercially by trawlers. Gulf of Alaska to central California.

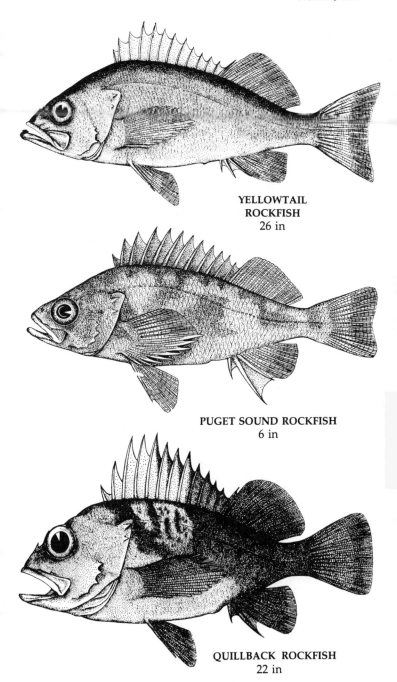

**YELLOWTAIL
ROCKFISH**
26 in

PUGET SOUND ROCKFISH
6 in

QUILLBACK ROCKFISH
22 in

■ Greenlings

Family Hexagrammidae

Small northern family of medium-size elongated fishes. Long, continuous dorsal fin notched at about the midpoint. Some have cirri (small, fleshy outgrowths) above eyes. Found near rocks and kelp. Tend to stay in small area. Found in shallow water (especially Lingcod during breeding season).

■ KELP GREENLING

Hexagrammos decagrammus

Distinctive color patterns; sexes differ. **Male:** Olive tinged with copper or blue. Front of body has large blue spots ringed by reddish brown spots. Head gets bluer during breeding season. Dark bars on dorsal fins; tinges of blue and white on pectoral and anal fins. **Female:** Mostly golden speckled with reddish brown. Reddish fins. Both sexes reach 24 inches, about 5 pounds.

Common in shallow areas near rocky shores; in kelp beds; and near jetties. Solitary bottom dweller; territorial when defending eggs. Male tends to live somewhat deeper than female. Active during day; hides at night. Feeds on variety of amphipods and other crustaceans, worms, and small fishes. Preyed on by seals and Lingcod, by human divers and anglers. Aleutian Islands to southern California.

■ WHITESPOTTED GREENLING

Hexagrammos stelleri

Small mouth; distinctive body shape; white spotting. Pointed head. Body thick near pectoral fins; slender toward rear. Background color variable: light brown to green; darker vertical bars or blotches on sides and fins. White spots. Yellowish anal fin. To 19 inches.

Common in shallow water among rocks or over gravel beaches, in kelp beds and Eelgrass; also found in deeper water. Feeds on amphipods, crabs, shrimps, worms, and small fishes. Spawns April; eggs blue. Japan to Alaska to Oregon.

■ LINGCOD

Ophiodon elongatus

Long slender body covered with dark spots. Pointed snout. Large mouth and caninelike teeth. Long, notched dorsal fin. Background color variable: shades of brown, gray, or green above; pale below. Juvenile gold with mottled brown. Our largest greenling; grows to 5 feet; over 80 pounds.

Common on or near reefs or kelp beds. Prefers deep water with strong current. In winter female lays eggs on or under rocks in shallow (even intertidal) water. Male guards, fans, and cleans pink egg masses (sometimes more than 1) for about 6 weeks. Aggressive during this time; will even push off dogfish. Do not disturb.

Juvenile feeds on plankton. Adult is voracious predator on many fishes, crabs, octopus, and even smaller lingcod. In turn, is eagerly sought by anglers and scuba divers; fishery is now regulated. Central Alaska to northern Baja California.

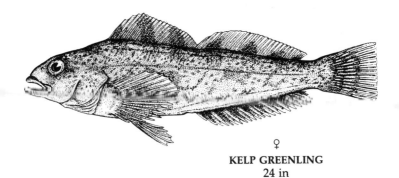

♀
KELP GREENLING
24 in

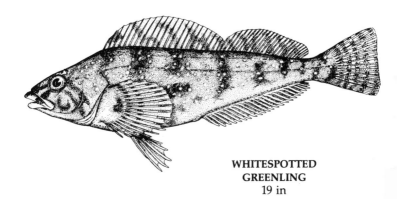

**WHITESPOTTED
GREENLING**
19 in

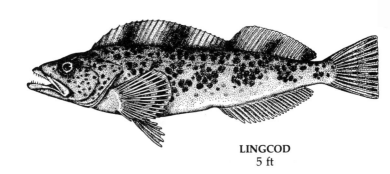

LINGCOD
5 ft

■ PAINTED GREENLING
Oxylebius pictus

Long, pointed head with 2 cirri. Tan background with 5 to 7 dark, reddish vertical bars across body and unpaired fins ("convict fish"). During summer breeding season female has more contrast; male darkens (except underneath, where it develops whitish blotches). To 10 inches.

Common near shore in sheltered water. Not shy. Slow moving but adult more active in summer. Elaborate courtship. Male actively defends egg masses (often of more than one female), especially against male of same species. Gulf of Alaska to southern California.

■ Sculpins
Family Cottidae

Blunt-headed, medium-size fish. Often rest on bottom on large, fan-like pectoral fins. Tend to be well camouflaged and sedentary; hide in crevices and among seaweeds waiting for prey. Some are among our most abundant fishes.

■ SAILFIN SCULPIN
Nautichthys oculofasciatus

Tall, separate first dorsal fin (sailfin). Broad, black diagonal stripe through eye. Pit on top of head behind eyes. Brown to gray above, lighter below. To 8 inches.

Common, but primarily nocturnal; hides in crevices during day. Seen at night over rocky and kelp-covered sandy bottoms. Undulates the long second dorsal fin when swimming. Alaska to southern California.

■ GRUNT SCULPIN
Rhamphocottus richardsoni

Unique, laterally compressed shape. Long snout separated from high ridged forehead. Yellowish with dark reddish brown diagonal streaks on sides. Lower rays of pectoral fins detached and elongated. To 3 inches.

Locally common. Found in tide pools and shallow water along rocky shores and around pilings; also over sand bottom and to depths. Swims with body higher than tail. Crawls or hops over rocks or seaweed on enlarged lower rays of pectoral fins. Often hides in large barnacle shells, bottles, and cans. Spawning female chases and traps male. Feeds on a variety of small crustaceans. Japan to Alaska to southern California.

■ ROUGHBACK SCULPIN
Chitonotus pugetensis

Tall, dark, slender segment at anterior of first dorsal fin, followed by a deep notch. Back and top of head covered with rough scales. Antler-like preopercular spine on gill covers. Dark green to brown above with 4 darker brown saddles; light below. In breeding season male has large, oddly shaped penis in front of anal fin; red blotch on side; head and fins turn dark on some. To 9 inches.

Common from intertidal to deep water. Nocturnal. Buries itself during day. Feeds on shrimp and other crustaceans, worms, and snails. Northern British Columbia to Baja California.

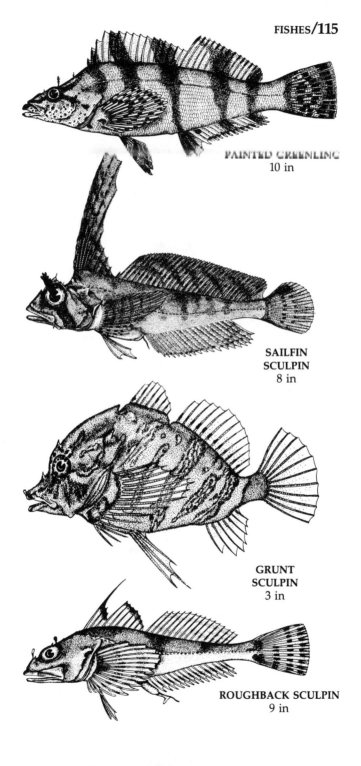

PAINTED GREENLING
10 in

SAILFIN
SCULPIN
8 in

GRUNT
SCULPIN
3 in

ROUGHBACK SCULPIN
9 in

■**TIDEPOOL SCULPIN**   *Oligocottus maculosus*
Pugnacious. Found in almost every tide pool. Color variable but
tends toward olive green, with irregular dark saddles and whitish V
or saddle across back. No prickles or scales. To 4 inches.

Tolerant of great changes in temperature, salinity, and oxygen
content; can even climb partly out of water for an extended period of
time. Catches tiny crustaceans and darts after pieces of larger animals
that fall into tide pool or shallows. Alaska to southern California.

A similar-looking sculpin found in tide pools is the **Fluffy Sculpin** (*Oligocottus snyderi*). Color variable; 4 to 6 dark saddles on back.
White spots under head. Male has long, separated first ray of anal
fin.

Another, smaller sculpin found in tide pools is the **Sharpnose
Sculpin** (*Clinocottus acuticeps*). Gray with chocolate brown spots on
back. Told by row of cirri on top of head and along lateral line; dark
bar on first dorsal fin.

■**PACIFIC STAGHORN SCULPIN**   *Leptocottus armatus*
Sharp, antlerlike spine on operculum (gill cover). Dark spot at rear of
first dorsal fin. Pectoral fin is barred. No scales. Head is large, flattened, and streamlined. To 18 inches.

Most abundant local sculpin; especially abundant in protected
bays and estuaries, from high tide levels to moderate depths over
muddy or sandy bottoms. When disturbed buries itself in sand or
mud up to eyes; if further threatened expands spined operculum.
Tolerates low salinities; sometimes found in lower portions of
streams. Feeds on a variety of isopods, worms, clam siphons, small
crustaceans, and small fishes. Preyed on by California Sea Lion,
cormorants. Bering Sea to Baja California.

■**SCALYHEAD SCULPIN**   *Artedius harringtoni*
Small. Rough scales on head. Big eyes. Flattened, skin-covered spine
on operculum (gill cover). Adult has orange under head. Brown to
olive above; dark saddles across back. Light spots on lower sides
blend into light belly. **Male:** Two small outgrowths (cirri) on head.
Brilliant gold under head; red rays from eyes. Large penis. **Female:**
Pink on pelvic and anal fins. To 4 inches.

Common around rocky reefs and pilings from depths of 15 to 35
feet. Male highly territorial during spawning season. Feeds on a great
variety of small benthic and pelagic organisms. Central Alaska to
southern California.

■**SMOOTHHEAD SCULPIN**   *Artedius lateralis*
Slender body. Pointed snout with small eyes; large mouth. Dorsal fin
divided into 2 parts. Greenish to brown above with about 6 dark
saddles on back. To 5 inches.

Common inter- and subtidally on all types of bottom except
mud. Egg masses (yellow-red) attached to rocks winter to spring.
Feeds on shrimps and other small crustaceans and on small fishes.
Alaska to Baja California.

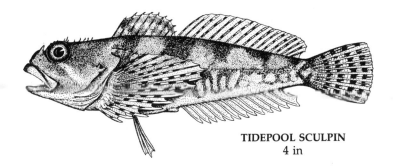

TIDEPOOL SCULPIN
4 in

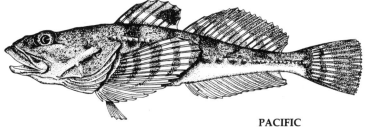

**PACIFIC
STAGHORN SCULPIN**
18 in

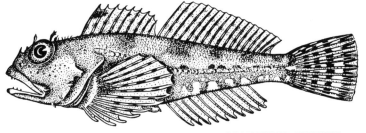

SCALYHEAD SCULPIN
4 in

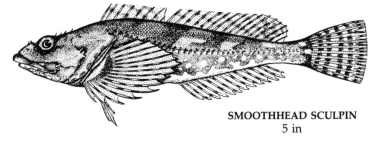

SMOOTHHEAD SCULPIN
5 in

■ BUFFALO SCULPIN
Enophyrys bison

Big, blunt, globular head with short, steep snout. Small, close-set eyes. Mostly greenish brown, lighter below. Large straight opercular spine on gill cover; large, raised plates along high lateral line. To 14 inches.

Abundant around rocks in shallow water. Smaller individuals are found over exposed gravel beaches. Adult spawns in spring near low tide line. Batches of eggs attached to rocks may be purple, pink, red, orange, yellow, or tan. Feeds on Sea Lettuce and a variety of small benthic animals. Often caught unintentionally by anglers. Avoid sharp opercular spines! Gulf of Alaska to central California.

■ RED IRISH LORD
Hemilepidotus hemilepidotus

Large eyes bulging from low, wide forehead. Two notches (the rearward deeper) in the single, long dorsal fin. Wide band of scales around dorsal fin. Color variable (depending on habitat): mottled reds and/or browns with spotting. Four or so dark saddles across back; sometimes white spot. Pectoral and anal fins have dark spotting. Dark bands across tail fin. To 20 inches.

Common in rocky kelp beds and shallows; colorful juveniles sometimes found in large tide pools. Adult eats crabs, isopods, barnacles, mussels, and small fishes. In March female attaches masses of pink eggs to mussels, barnacles, and rocks in strong current. She (or both parents) guards egg mass from predators. Soviet Union to Alaska to central California.

■ GREAT SCULPIN
Myoxocephalus polyacanthocephalus

Large spine on operculum (gill cover). Elongated, wide head. Distinguished from Buffalo Sculpin by large mouth and lack of plates along nearly invisible lateral line. Deep olive above, pale below; 4 dark saddles across back. To 30 inches.

Common on sand or rock bottom at shallow to moderate depths. Feeds on snails, amphipods, and other small crustaceans. Japan to Alaska to Puget Sound.

■ CABEZON
Scorpaenichthys marmoratus

No scales. Large, bushy cirri above each eye. Skin flap on snout. Color variable, brown, reddish or olive green above with numerous large blotches of lighter green. One of our largest sculpins. To over 30 inches, 15 pounds.

Commonly encountered by divers in rocky areas, near wrecks, and in kelp beds. Adult spawns during winter. Red eggs laid in large masses on rocks or seaweed; intertidal to subtidal. Juvenile (found near shore) is often splotched shades of pink and red; blends with pink encrusting algae. Feeds on isopods, crustaceans, fishes, and mollusks. Hunted by scuba divers and anglers. Eggs are toxic! Southeastern Alaska to Baja California.

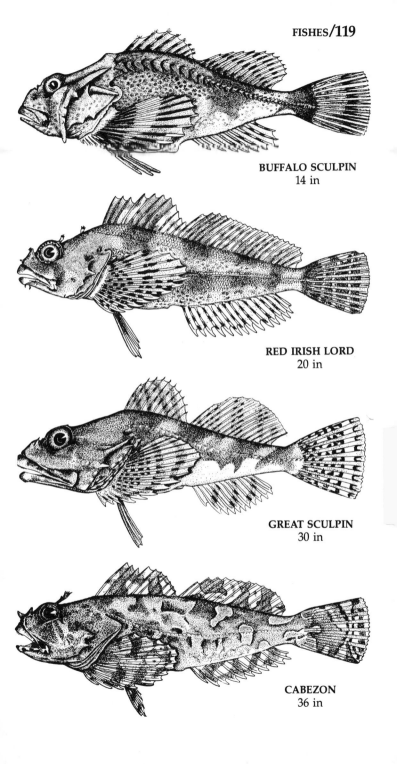

BUFFALO SCULPIN
14 in

RED IRISH LORD
20 in

GREAT SCULPIN
30 in

CABEZON
36 in

■ Poachers
Family Agonidae

Small, slender fishes covered with hard, spiny plates. Two dorsal fins. Undulate pectoral fins to swim. Most species found at moderate depths over muddy bottom.

■ STURGEON POACHER
Agonus acipenserinus

Rows of bony plates cover slender body. Resembles miniature sturgeon. Told from other poachers by pointed, flattened snout that overhangs the mouth; clusters of yellow cirri hanging from under snout. Grayish tan with dark blotches above; golden below. Orange spot under eye. Dark base of tail fin. Largest local poacher. To 12 inches.

Found at shallow to moderate depths on soft bottoms. Feeds primarily on amphipods, copepods, and shrimps. Alaska to northern California.

■ NORTHERN SPEARNOSE POACHER
Agonopsis vulsa

Bony scales. Told from other poachers by pair of blunt spines at tip of snout; transparent spot on tail fin. Tan above with darker blotches; light below. Pelvic fin dark brown with white tip. Thin stripes on tail fin. To 8 inches.

Common from shallow to moderate depths. Life history little known. Southeastern Alaska to southern California.

■ PYGMY POACHER
Odontopyxis trispinosa

Told from species above by smaller size; small head and short snout; relatively smooth scales; groove on back behind head. One sharp vertical spine (and sometimes 2 lateral ones) on top of snout. Grayish tan to olive with darker blotches above; light below. To 3 inches.

Common but inconspicuous. Southeastern Alaska to Baja California.

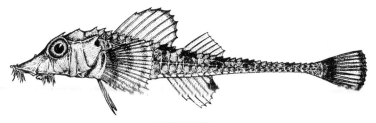

**STURGEON
POACHER**
12 in

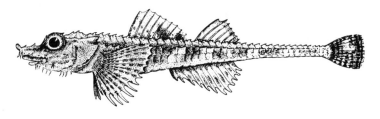

**NORTHERN
SPEARNOSE POACHER**
8 in

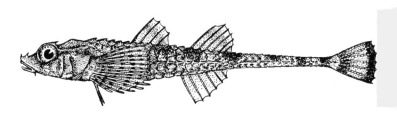

**PYGMY
POACHER**
3 in

■Righteye Flounders, Soles, and Halibut

Family Pleuronectidae

Familiar, flattened bottom fishes. Larva looks normal, with long dorsal and anal fins. Left eye, as it develops, migrates around head and ends up higher than right eye. Right-sided from then on, with eyed (right) side facing up (except some Starry Flounders). Blind side becomes pale and loses scales. Food on worms, clams, thin siphons, brittle stars, shrimps, and other small benthic organisms.

Most species live on or partly buried in sandy or muddy substrate. Juveniles commonly found in shallows (preyed on by Great Blue Heron, gulls, and River Otter). Adults tend to move into deeper water. Most species spawn November to June.

■STARRY FLOUNDER

Platichthys stellatus

Broad orange and black stripes on large fins. Body sharply pointed in front, wide in center. Arrowhead shape accentuated by triangular dorsal and anal fins. Tail fin somewhat rounded. Unlike most flounders, can be either left- or right-sided. Eyed side is dark gray, brown, or green and vaguely blotched; blind side is white. Grows to 36 inches, 20 pounds.

Common in shallows on varied substrates. Tolerates fresh water; abundant around river mouths and estuaries. Juvenile feeds on small crustaceans; adds worms to diet as it ages. An important sport fish. Japan to Bering Sea to southern California.

■PACIFIC HALIBUT

Hippoglossus stenolepis

Largest flounder. Slightly forked tail fin. Center of dorsal and anal fins somewhat pointed. Mouth large and agape. Eyes raised. Lateral line has secondary bump near end of pectoral fin before straightening. Brown-gray with lighter blotches; blind side white. Body thick and meaty. Female reaches over 8 feet, 450 pounds. Male to 4.5 feet, 120 pounds. Most caught locally are juveniles; average about 35 pounds.

Locally common in Strait of Juan de Fuca and seaward; occasionally into inner Puget Sound. Adult most common at depths greater than 300 feet. Great size has made it most important commercial and sport bottom fish since local Indians first developed technology to hook it. Japan to Bering Sea to southern California.

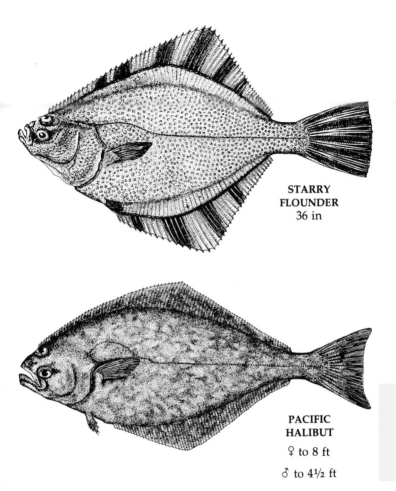

**STARRY
FLOUNDER**
36 in

**PACIFIC
HALIBUT**
♀ to 8 ft
♂ to 4½ ft

■ROCK SOLE
Lepidopsetta bilineata

Rounded shape exaggerated by dorsal and anal fins (which are blotched). Lateral line has high arch over pectoral fin and short accessory branch. Rough scales. Color variable: mottled gray to reddish brown. To about 24 inches.

Abundant. Found in 30- to 150-foot depths over rubble, shell, or pebble bottom. Feeds on worms, amphipods, clams, and crabs. Common sport fish. Japan to Bering Sea to southern California.

■FLATHEAD SOLE
Hippoglossoides elassodon

Large mouth with single row of teeth in upper jaw. Very flattened; juvenile especially thin. Lateral line straight from tip of pectoral fin. Tail fin straight or slightly rounded. Gray-brown, sometimes blotched with darker brown. To 18 inches.

Common in bays over mud bottom at depths of 60 to 150 feet. Not an important commercial or sport fish. Japan to Alaska to central California.

■BUTTER SOLE
Isopsetta isolepsis

Oval shape. Gray and blotched; sometimes with green and yellow spots. Dorsal and anal fins tipped with bright yellow. Rounded tail fin. Rough scales. Male to 15 inches. Female to 18 inches.

Common on muddy bottom in sheltered bays. Bering Sea to southern California.

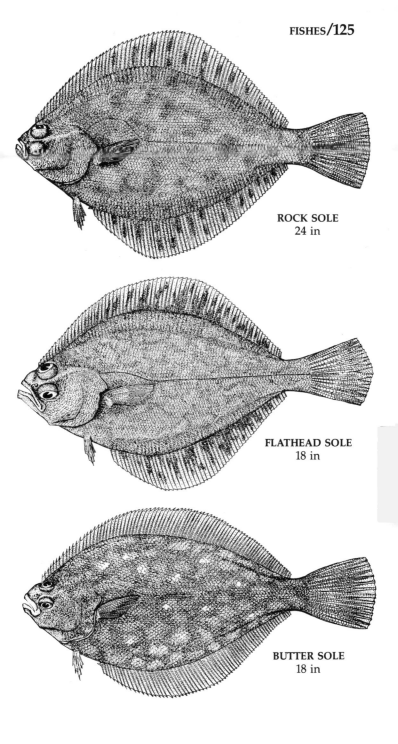

ROCK SOLE
24 in

FLATHEAD SOLE
18 in

BUTTER SOLE
18 in

■ C-O SOLE
Pleuronichthys coenosus

Raised eyes, so close set they almost touch. Shape appears very round due to rounded dorsal and anal fins. Tough skin. Color variable: very dark to sandy and blotched. Dark spot in center of body. Dark sickle and dot on rounded tail fin (especially of juvenile) give species the name C-O. To 14 inches.

Abundant in wide variety of habitats. Adult found at depths to low 60 feet; juvenile in shallower water in summer. Feeds on isopods, amphipods, worms, small fishes, and small clams. Southeastern Alaska to northern Baja California.

■ SAND SOLE
Psettichthys melanostictus

Long free rays on front end of dorsal fin. Tail fin somewhat squared. Large mouth. Eyed side varies from brown to green; speckled with fine black points. To 25 inches.

Common and widespread in shallow water over clean sand. Feeds on amphipods and other benthic crustaceans and worms. A good sport fish. Bering Sea to southern California.

■ ENGLISH SOLE
Parophrys vetulus

Distinctly long, narrow, pointed head with small mouth. Eyed side smooth on front end (except cheeks), rough on rear end. Lateral line barely bends above pectoral fin. Eyed side uniformly brown; blind side yellowish tinged with reddish brown. Long fins same color as body, but translucent. To about 20 inches.

Our most common flounder in shallows; also found in deep water. Moves deeper as it ages and deeper in winter, more shallow in spring. Feeds on amphipods, copepods, mysids, worms, and small clams. An important commercial, sport, and research fish; sensitive to polluted sediments. Bering Sea to central Baja California.

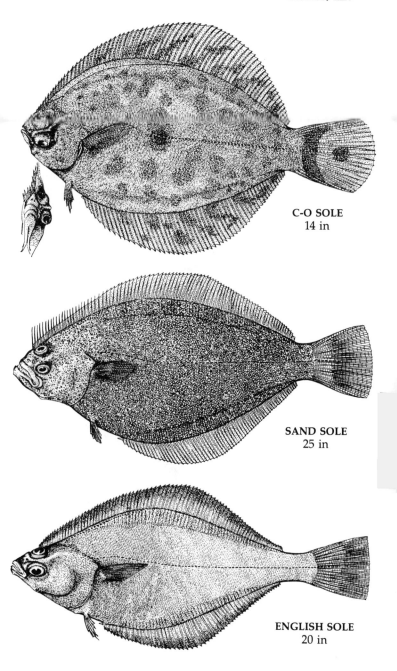

C-O SOLE
14 in

SAND SOLE
25 in

ENGLISH SOLE
20 in

■**SLENDER SOLE**   *Lyopsetta exilis*
Slender body. Rounded tail fin. Large mouth. Large scales fall off
easily. Lateral line does not arch. Pale brown with fine black speckling. To 14 inches.
        Common and widespread on muddy sand bottoms in shallow to
moderate depth. Southeastern Alaska to Baja California.

■ **REX SOLE**   *Glyptocephalus zachirus*
Long, slender, dark pectoral fin on eyed side of body. Straight lateral
line. Slender, thin body. Tiny mouth. Adult is a uniformly light
brown; juvenile is translucent. To 23 inches.
        Adult is common in deep water. Juvenile common in moderately
deep water; less so in shallows. Considered too thin for commercial
fish processing; not an important sport fish. Bering Sea to southern
California.

■**DOVER SOLE**   *Microstomus pacificus*
Bulging eyes. Tiny mouth. Straight lateral line barely bends above
pectoral fin. Eyed side mottled brown. Blind side light to dark gray,
sometimes blotched with dull red. Fins have dusky edge. Rounded
tail fin. Body is flaccid when out of water; covered with thick layer of
slime. To 30 inches.
        Common at moderate depths over muddy bottom. An important
commercial fish. Bering Sea to central Baja California.

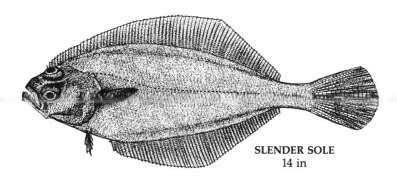

SLENDER SOLE
14 in

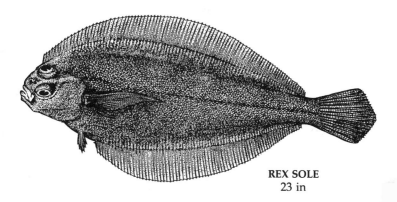

REX SOLE
23 in

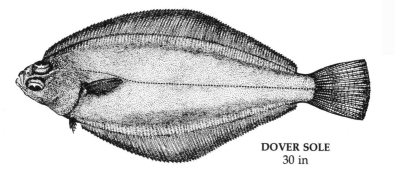

DOVER SOLE
30 in

■ Sanddabs
Family Bothidae

Also called lefteye or left-sided flounders because right eye migrates to left side of body. Otherwise similar to flounders and soles.

■ SPECKLED SANDDAB
Citharichthys stigmaeus

Olive brown; finely speckled with black dots. Creamy on blind side. Juvenile sandy and translucent. Short tail; rear edge of dorsal fin almost reaches rounded tail fin. To 6 inches.

Common over sand bottoms in shallow water. Feeds on worms, amphipods, and other benthic organisms. Southeastern Alaska to southern Baja California.

■ PACIFIC SANDDAB
Citharichthys sordidus

Resembles Speckled Sanddab, but has squared-off tail and larger eyes. To 16 inches.

Common on sand below 50-foot depth. Feeds on amphipods, mysids, shrimps, and worms. Considered an important year-round sport fish. Bering Sea to southern Baja California.

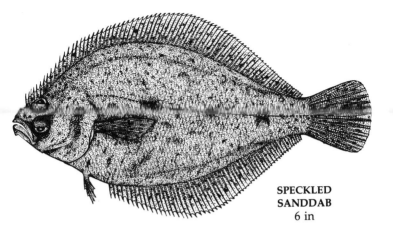

**SPECKLED
SANDDAB**
6 in

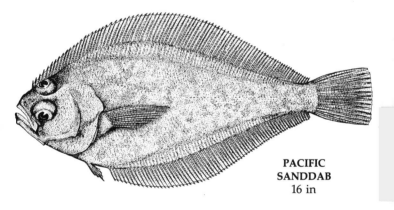

**PACIFIC
SANDDAB**
16 in

INVERTEBRATES

▌███ Sponges   *Phylum* Porifera

Considered the most primitive of multi-celled animals; no special-ized tissues such as nervous system or blood. Collar cells (choano-cytes) with whiplike flagella create a current through tiny incurrent pores (ostia). Microscopic plankton are filtered from water before it exits through large excurrent pores (oscula). Most cells contain hard fibers (spicules) that give the sponge shape. Most species are perma-nently attached to rocks, wood, and shells; most local ones are simple, soft, encrusting types.

■ BREAD CRUMB SPONGE   *Halichondria panicea*

Soft, encrusting sponge. Tan, yellow, or light green. To 2 inches thick; uneven, often ridged. Tends to be thicker than Haliclona (be-low); excurrent "volcanoes" not as large and raised. Breadlike tex-ture. When broken, smells like exploded gunpowder. Found from low tide to moderate depths. Grazed by dorid nudibranchs.

A related species of encrusting sponge, **Halichondria bowerbanki,** tends to grow thinner. Found on floats.

■ RED SPONGE   *Ophlitaspongia pennata*

Grows in thin patches. Bright red or red-orange. Pores are starlike and closely packed. Common under intertidal rocks in shallow sub-tidal zone; prefers strong wave action. Grazed by tiny Red Nudi-branch, which matches its color perfectly.

■ HALICLONA   *Haliclona* sp.

Surface covered with many large, volcanolike excurrent pores (with openings up to ¼ inch); thousands of tiny incurrent pores. Gray, violet, or brown. Common encrusting sponge; grows on floats, rocks, seaweeds. Tends to be thinner than Bread Crumb Sponge; crushed, it doesn't smell like expoloded gunpowder. Found from midtide to shallow subtidal. Grazed by Ringed Doris and other dorid nudibranchs.

■ BORING SPONGE   *Cliona celata*

Forms yellow patches on shells of Rock Scallop, barnacles, oysters, and clams. Below the shell surface, specialized sponge cells secrete sulfuric acid to dissolve shell. Helps break down discarded shells on sea floor.

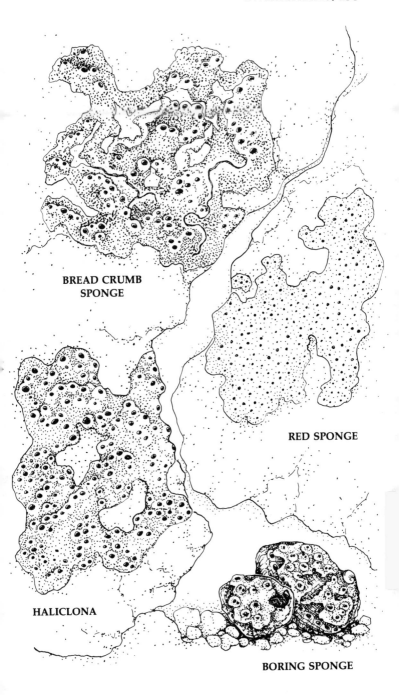

BREAD CRUMB
SPONGE

RED SPONGE

HALICLONA

BORING SPONGE

▪▪▪▪ Cnidarians (Coelenterates)   *Phylum* Cnidaria

Phylum include hydroids, scyphozoan jellyfishes, sea anemones, sea pens, and corals. Constructed of 2 layers of cells—the outer covering and the inner lining of digestive cavity. Between is jellylike layer (mesoglea). Some cells specialized for digesting or stinging. Some species are colonial.

Many species have alternate generations—"polyp" stage is sessile (connected to substrate), free-swimming "medusa" stage is called jellyfish. Hydrozoan jellies are usually tiny; some scyphozoan jellies are quite large. Both are common locally in spring and summer, rare in winter.

Cnidarians have true mouths and stomachs. In jellyfishes, they hang together from center of bell on a stalk (manubrium). Tentacles hang from lower edge of bell. At base of tentacles are small balance organs (statocysts). Within tentacles are stinging cells (nematocysts) used for protection and to paralyze prey.

▪▪▪▪ Hydroids   *Class* Hydrozoa

Alternate generations. Vegetative "polyp stage" grows on rocks, shells, sea plants, floats, and pilings. Sexual "medusa stage" is small jellyfish. Hydroid medusa has membrane (velum) that grows inward from margin of the bell. Most of the 60 or so local jellyfishes are medusae of hydrozoans; are surprisingly attractive, but usually very small and go unnoticed.

▪ WATER JELLYFISH   *Aequorea victoria*

Our largest hydrozoan jelly by far (to 5 inches in diameter). Transparent bell is thick and gelatinous; underparts are lined with 50 to 150 radial canals. An equal number of long slender tentacles hang from margin of bell. Perhaps the most luminescent of our larger jellyfishes; glows in the dark when touched.

▪ OBELIA   *Obelia geniculata*

Dominant polyp stage forms fuzzy white patches on floats and on Eelgrass. Mossy colonies are composed of thousands of specialized feeding and reproductive polyps on branching stalks. Feeding polyps have stinging cells (nematocysts), which explode and harpoon tiny prey organisms. Tiny medusae bud off from reproductive cells.

A related hydroid, *Obelia dichotoma,* forms beardlike colonies, a foot or so long, that hang from floats.

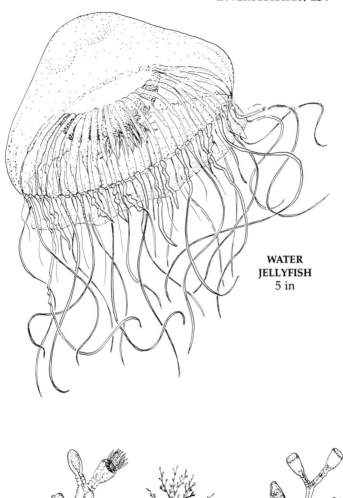

**WATER
JELLYFISH**
5 in

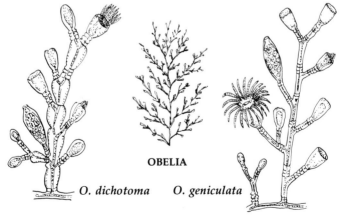

OBELIA

O. dichotoma   *O. geniculata*

▇▇▇Large Jellyfishes
Class Scyphozoa

Our large jellyfishes are medusa stage of scyphozoans; common ones are usually at least 4 inches in diameter. Polyp stage (scyphistoma) looks like miniature sea anemone; medusae form budlike stack of saucers from tip of polyp.

■MOON JELLY
Aurelia aurita

Common large clear jellyfish. Floats near surface; washes up on beaches in great numbers in some years. Bell is firm and flattened. To 6 inches or more. Four semicircular gonads (white or tinged with color) form cloverleaf pattern seen near center of transparent bell. Radial canals branch toward margins, which have 8 shallow lobes; sense organs lie between lobes. Numerous tiny tentacles fringe the margin. Some people are sensitive to mild sting of nematocysts. Uses sticky mucus to capture tiny planktonic organisms.

■LION'S MANE
Cyanea capillata

World's largest jellyfish and by far the largest locally. Arctic specimens reach 8 feet in diameter; local ones may reach 24 inches. Muscular bell is transparent. Huge, frilly manubrium beneath bell is usually tawny, hence "lion's mane"; larger specimens tend toward purplish red. Eight groups of tentacles hanging from margin; extended, they can trail 6 feet below bell.

Often seen in large numbers in late summer; many end up stranded on beaches. Even when beached, tentacles can deliver nasty sting, hence the other common name "sea nettle." Heads of quiet bays sometimes fill with invisible stinging tentacles.

LION'S MANE
24 in

MOON JELLY
6 in

■■■Sea Anemones
Class Anthozoa

Class includes corals and sea fans. No alternation of generations—all are polyps. Anemones attach by "pedal disk" to rock, shell, or piling; many species can slowly glide, crawl, or burrow if necessary.

■BROODING ANEMONE
Epiactis prolifera

Small (to 1½ inches tall, 2 inches wide). Color variable: olive, green, or purple on Eelgrass or algae; sometimes pink to red on rocks. White lines radiate out from center of oral disk. About 100 short, tapered tentacles.

Usually found attached to Eelgrass or seaweed in quiet bays. The tiny anemones found on disk or body were fertilized in gut; settled outside as larvae. Protected by parent's tentacles until moving off on their own.

■ELEGANT (Aggregating) ANEMONE
Anthopleura elegantissima

Small (less than 2 inches). Very common on rocks, in tide pools, or in sand-covered patches. Olive green body nondescript when closed up, but truly elegant when slender, shapely, pink-tipped tentacles are extended. Often divides to form dense colonies of clones. Individuals of same colony tolerate close contact, but clone colonies coming into contact sting each other with specialized capsules; create "no-man's-land" between.

Feeds on small crustaceans and other organisms. Also ingests single-celled green algae, which give greenish color.

■GREEN ANEMONE
Anthopleura xanthogrammica

Short, wide (to 6 inches). Body column dark olive. Broad oral disk and short, thick, tapered tentacles are emerald green. Color derives from single-celled algae, which are ingested and remain alive. Fish and crustaceans are paralyzed and enclosed by tentacles; mussels and other animals are washed onto the oral disk by surf. Found only in exposed areas.

■RED AND GREEN ANEMONE
Urticina (Tealia) crassicornis

Hundred or so tentacles are fairly short, wider at base than tip; tan to greenish, or reddish, or with bands of red. Body is stocky. Color variable: sometimes entirely tan, olive, or bright red; often streaked with bright reds and greens. Common in tide pools or hanging sac-like under rocks. Intertidal to 5 inches; subtidal to 10 inches. May live 60 years.

The related *Urticina coriacea* is found in gravel, mud, or crushed shell. Disk is attached to rock beneath; only upper third of tall body exposed. Bright red, with some tan or gray. Tentacles stubby and cylindrical; usually pink in the middle, lighter above, darker below.

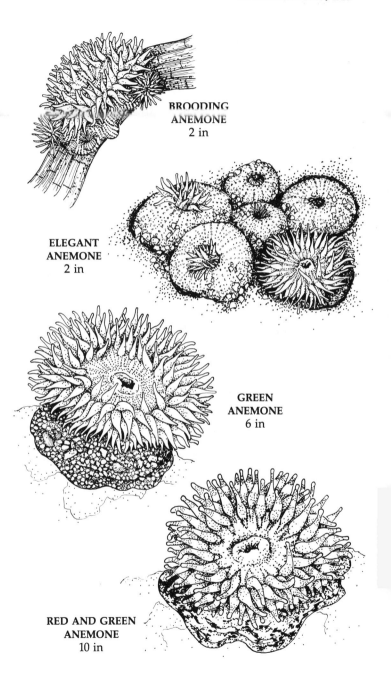

**BROODING
ANEMONE**
2 in

**ELEGANT
ANEMONE**
2 in

**GREEN
ANEMONE**
6 in

**RED AND GREEN
ANEMONE**
10 in

■**PLUMED (Frilled) ANEMONE**   *Metridium* sp.
Tall, white, cylindrical body. More than 200 slender white tentacles
form feathery plume to filter tiny animals from plankton. Large subtidal specimen may grow 24 or more inches tall. Lives many years.

Sometimes found intertidally, but much more common on floats
(tolerates poor water quality and low salinity); subtidally on pilings
and rocks. Thick growths transform old piers and pilings into Roman
columns and ghostly gardens.

The closely related **Small Metridium,** *Metridium senile*—illustrated
in circle—until recently was considered a form of the Plumed Anemone; now is given full species status. It is much shorter (to 2 inches).
The column is brownish; the many thin tentacles are white to tan. Often a thick white ring around the mouth on the oral disk. Found on
floats and piers, and subtidally on hard objects in quiet bays.

■**SEA PEN**   *Ptilosarcus gurneyi*
When expanded, looks like huge, orange feather (about 18 inches
high) with swollen quill. Actually it is a colony of smaller animals,
closely related to sea anemones. "Plumes" are composed of 20 or so
pairs of branches, each bearing hundreds of feeding polyps. Fleshy
stem is composed of polyps that force water through the colony.

Found subtidally, often just below lowest tide; embedded in
mud or sand bottom. Often forms dense aggregations. Can contract
into the mud when disturbed. Luminesces in the dark or when disturbed. A major source of food for many sea stars and nudibranchs.

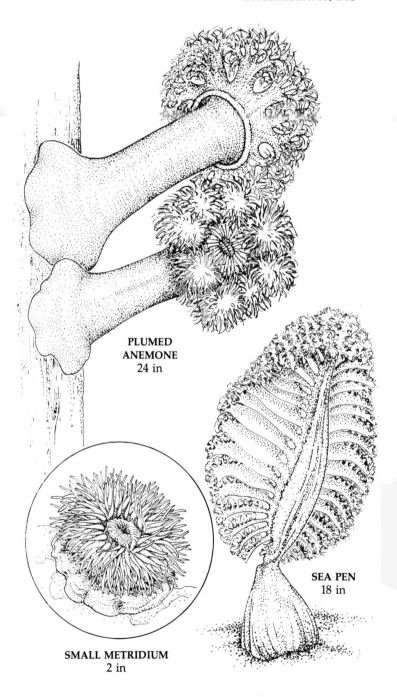

**PLUMED
ANEMONE**
24 in

SEA PEN
18 in

SMALL METRIDIUM
2 in

▮▮▮▮**Flatworms** *Phylum* Platyhelminthes

Unsegmented. Primitive; lack blood or circulatory system. But reproductive systems are complex and heads have pair of eyes. Capable of simple learning. Most are small and flat; leaf-shaped when contracted, ribbonlike when outstretched. Phylum includes three classes: flukes, tapeworms, and turbellarians (marine flatworms).

▮▮▮▮Polyclad Marine Flatworms *Class* Turbellaria

Order Polycladida

Common in sand and mud, under rocks, or on seaweed. Most are very small and go unnoticed. Glide along on thousands of tiny cilia. Some graze on diatoms; others prey on tiny zooplankton.

▮LEAF WORM *Kaburakia excelsa*

Our largest polyclad worm; to 4 inches when extended. Found gliding over seaweeds and mussel beds and under rocks. Orange to brown. When contracted, the thin edges are frilly. Tiny black spots along margin are eyespots; also has eyespots on small tentacles near front. Preys on tiny benthic organisms.

Most other local flatworms are much smaller; most larger common species are of the genus *Notoplana*.

▮▮▮▮**Nemerteans** *Phylum* Nemertea

Long and slender; but very contractile. Break apart easily. More advanced than flatworms; have circulatory system. Retractable proboscis has either sticky glands or poisonous needles, both used for capturing prey.

▮ORANGE NEMERTEAN *Tubulanus polymorphus*

Our largest and most spectacular nemertean. Can reach 3 feet in length when fully extended but, like other nemerteans, is usually partially contracted. Bright red-orange. Tubular in shape. Lacks eye spots on head. Found in exposed rocky situations.

▮GREEN NEMERTEAN *Emplectonema gracile*

Found on exposed beaches; coiled in mussel beds or seaweed-covered rocks. Green above; whitish or yellowish below. Eyespots on head. Fully contracted, it is thick and only an inch or so long; fully extended, it is very slender and can reach 5 inches. Usually some sections are contracted while others are extended.

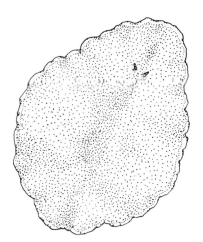

LEAF WORM
4 in

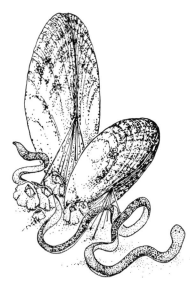

GREEN NEMERTEAN
5 in

ORANGE NEMERTEAN
36 in

■ **THICK AMPHIPORUS**   *Amphiporus bimaculatus*
Short but stout. To about 5 inches. Brownish red or orange. Triangular markings on lighter head. Usually found beneath or between rocks.

■ **THIN AMPHIPORUS**   *Amphiporus imparispinosus* and
                                          Amphiporus formidabilis
Both species are common on intertidal rocks among barnacles, mussels, and seaweed. Pale pink or whitish. *Amphiporus imparispinosus* is slender and tubular; to about 3 inches. *Amphiporus formidabilis* is similar but can reach 12 inches.

■ **MUD NEMERTEAN**   *Paranemertes perigrina*
Found crawling around on surface of muddy bays, usually where there is plenty of Sea Lettuce. Muddy purple above, pale yellow below. Reaches 6 inches when fully extended. Feeds on polychaete worms.

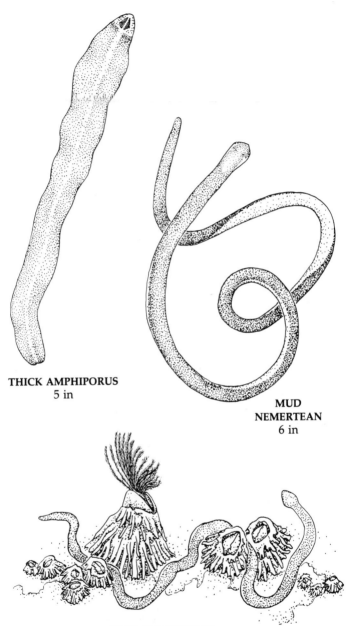

THICK AMPHIPORUS
5 in

**MUD
NEMERTEAN**
6 in

THIN AMPHIPORUS
12 in

▄▄▄ Segmented Worms

Phylum Annelida

Phylum includes earthworms, leeches, and polychaete marine worms.

▄▄▄ Marine Worms

Class Polychaeta

Large and varied class. Some are free swimming; some burrow in mud like earthworms; some of our most spectacular species live in tube a the y secrete in communit from mud or sand.

Distinct head (often with complex mouthparts) at one end, anus at the other. Trunk is divided into numerous identical body segments, each with pair of external flaps (parapodia). Paddle-shaped parapodia help "errant" species swim; bristly ones help burrowing species move through mud. Parapodia of tube dwellers are absent or much reduced.

Swimming and crawling polychaetes often have jaws or a large retractable proboscis, which everts to grab prey. Tube worms are mostly filter feeders; mouthparts are developed into large, feathery tentacles that act as gills and as nets to catch planktonic animals.

Polychaete tube worms are divided into three main families: Sabellids secrete leathery tubes and have feathery tentacles; Terebellids have many long, slender tentacles; Serpulids build hard, calcareous tubes.

▄▄▄ Nereid Worms

Family Nereidae

▄ SAND WORM

Nereis vexillosa

One of our largest marine worms (to 6 inches or more). Found on or just below surface of muddy beaches, or under rocks, or crawling through mussel beds. Muddy gray with oily iridescence. Jaws, when everted (which can be encouraged by carefully pressing behind the head section), are sharp, black pincers. Used for ripping seaweeds and for grabbing small creatures, including other worms. Periodically during summer, the sand worm's paddlelike parapodia expand, and it swims to the surface at night to mate in huge swarms.

The similar *Nereis brandti* grows from 1 to 3 feet long. It burrows deep in mud but may be seen when swarming.

▄▄▄ Lugworms

Family Arenicolidae

▄ LUGWORM

Abarenicola pacifica

Performs same function in muddy tideflats that earthworm does on land; passes mud through gut; digests bacteria and organic detritus. Most often spotted by its fecal castings: slender coils of mud near opening to J-shaped burrow. Color is muddy to fleshy; but branched gills (about a third back from head) are bright red. To 4 inches or more.

Another, larger lugworm, *Abarenicola claparedi,* is often found in clean sand. May reach 6 inches.

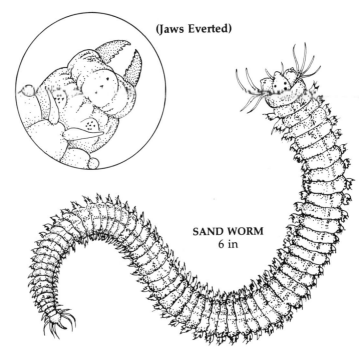

(Jaws Everted)

SAND WORM
6 in

LUGWORM
4 in

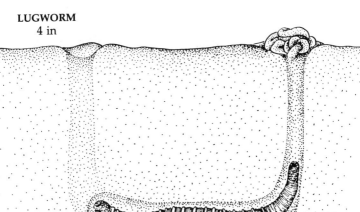

■ Sabellid Tube Worms
Family Sabellidae

Secrete leathery or parchmentlike tube. Feathery tentacles trap plankton; transported to mouth by wavelike action of thousands of tiny cilia along the plumes.

■ PLUME (Feather Duster) WORM
Schizobranchia insignis

Lives in clumps of leathery tubes attached to rocks, floats, or pilings. Tubes to about 8 inches; thickness of a pencil. When extended, the branching, feathery cirri form thick plume. May be red, orange, or various other colors. From lowest tide to subtidal. Common in harbors and marinas.

■ SMALL FEATHER DUSTER WORM
Potamilla occelata

Smallest of our 3 large plumed worms (to about 7 inches). Finely divided cirri are tan with noticeable eyespots; unbranched but split near the ends. Found on floats, pilings, and protected rocky beaches.

■ FEATHER DUSTER WORM
Eudistylia vancouveri

Tubes are somewhat thicker and longer (to 10 inches) than those of *Schizobranchia*. Feathery cirri are unbranched; alternately banded with maroon and green (sometimes tipped with blue). Cirri have eyespots that are light sensitive; a passing shadow will cause quick retraction. Found in crevices on rocky shores at lowest tide levels; also on floats or pilings.

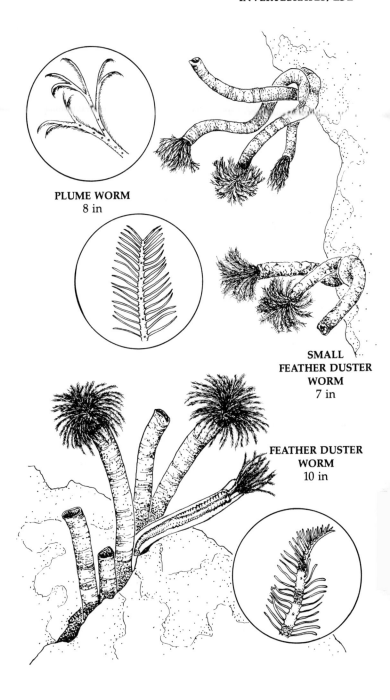

PLUME WORM
8 in

**SMALL
FEATHER DUSTER
WORM**
7 in

**FEATHER DUSTER
WORM**
10 in

■ Terebellid Tube Worms
Family Terebellidae

Construct leathery or sandy tubes. Long, slender tentacles convey tiny food particles to mouth.

■ SPAGHETTI WORM
Thelepus crispus

Long, exceedingly slender, white tentacles spread out over rocks or mud; food particles stick to tentacles and are moved by tiny cilia to the mouth. Tentacles can be quickly retracted. Pinkish body, with 3 pairs of red gills. To 6 inches. Abundant on rock or cobble beaches. Enclosed in long, sand-encrusted tubes; commonly found on the undersides of intertidal rocks. Tubes are fragile; the worm, like other organisms that live under rocks, may die if rock is not carefully returned to original position.

A similar spaghetti worm, *Eupolymnia heterobranchia,* is found on muddy sand beaches. Dark or greenish brown. Parchmentlike tube covered with sand grains.

■ Serpulids
Family Serpulidae

Construct hard tubes from calcium carbonate. Feathery tentacles are used as gills and for trapping planktonic animals.

■ CALCAREOUS TUBE WORM
Serpula vermicularis

Hard, curvy tubes are gray to lime white. Common under intertidal rocks, on shells and pilings, and on top of subtidal rocks. Worm itself is pink or flesh colored, with 40 pairs of pink gills. From 2 to 4 inches long. Cirri plumes are bright red. "Operculum," which blocks opening of tube when cirri retract, is red and shaped like a golf tee.

■ TINY TUBE WORM
Spirorbis spp.

Several species in genus. Common at lowest tide levels and abundant in subtidal zone. Tubular shell is coiled in a flat spiral (some species clockwise, some counterclockwise). Less than ¼ inch diameter. Circular plumes are red; look like a miniature version of Calcareous Tube Worm. A golf tee-shaped operculum blocks opening of tube when cirri retract.

■ Lamp Shells
Phylum Brachiopoda

Brachiopods resemble small, stalked clams; but differ internally and are not related to mollusks.

■ LAMP SHELL
Terebratalia transversa

Resembles Aladdin's lamp. About 1 inch wide. Clamlike; but hinged valves are unequal; cover top and bottom of animal rather than left and right sides. Attaches by tiny stalk. Our only common intertidal brachiopod. Common at minus tide levels in San Juan and Canadian Gulf islands. Most are unribbed but one variant is strongly ribbed.

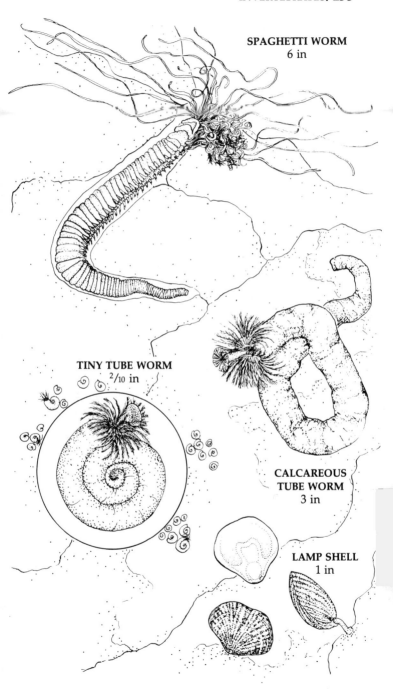

SPAGHETTI WORM
6 in

TINY TUBE WORM
$^2/_{10}$ in

CALCAREOUS TUBE WORM
3 in

LAMP SHELL
1 in

■■■■ Mollusks   *Phylum* Mollusca

One of the oldest, largest, and most successful groups of marine animals. Diverse. Divided into 6 classes; the 4 principal ones are: chitons; univalves (snails); bivalves (clams, mussels, scallops, etc.); and cephalopods (octopus and squid).

Most mollusks have a head, a visceral mass (body), and a muscular foot but bivalves lack a distinct head. Most mollusks are covered by one or more shells (valves); shell is secreted by glands in the "mantle," a soft or leathery covering of the inner organs. Most mollusks breathe with feathery gills that grow inside the mantle cavity. Nudibranchs (sea slugs) are exceptional—they do not have a shell, and they breath through projections from the body surface.

■■■■ Chitons   *Class* Amphineura

Primitive mollusks that lack tentacles; most species lack eyes. Shell is divided into eight shelly valves. Valves are surrounded and held together by a leathery outcrop of the mantle (girdle). On underside is a large snaillike foot on which the chiton glides slowly over rocks at night to feed or clamps to rocks in daylight. Most species graze on seaweeds or on film of diatoms and bacteria covering rocks and seaweeds, using a rasping tongue (radula).

■ GIANT PACIFIC (Gumboot)
CHITON   *Cryptochiton stelleri*

World's largest chiton; to 12 inches. Leathery, gray-to-orange or reddish brown girdle completely covers the 8 butterfly-shaped valves. Clings loosely to rocks; when handled curls like an armadillo. Often has a flesh-colored scale worm (*Arctinoe*) living under its mantle. Mostly subtidal but often found on rocky beaches at lowest tide levels.

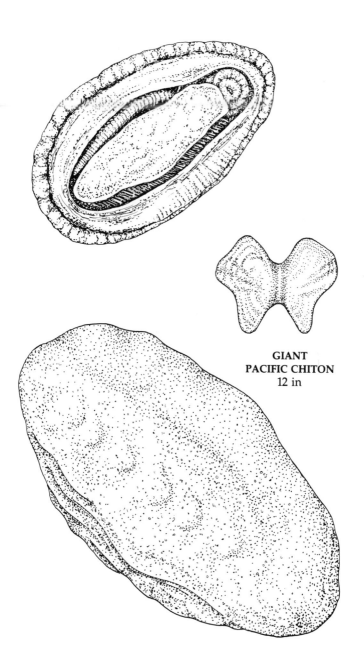

**GIANT
PACIFIC CHITON**
12 in

■MOSSY CHITON

Mopalia muscosa

Oval to oblong. Greenish gray girdle is covered with stiff, dark hairs. Valves are barely covered by mantle, but are often encrusted; a whitish line runs down center of valves. To 4 inches. Found on rocky shores and cobble beaches; in tide pools or clinging to undersides of rocks.

The **Hairy Chiton** (*Mopalia lignosa*) is similar in size and shape to the Mossy Chiton, but its valves are darker, and the hairs on girdle are much softer. The rasping tongue (radula) of both *Mopalia* species contains magnetite, an oxide or iron, and is particularly hard. Both species graze on film of diatoms and small animals growing on rocks.

■LINED CHITON

Tonicella lineata

Small. Exquisitely etched with pink and white lines and triangles; luminous green spots around mantle. Mostly subtidal. Grazes on upper layers of encrusting coralline algae, ingesting the film of diatoms and small animals on the algae. Thus it freshens the algae's colors, aiding its own camouflage.

■BLACK CHITON (Black Katy)

Katharina tunicata

The most abundant chiton on exposed rocky beaches. Smooth, black girdle covers all but the center of the 8 gray valves. To 4 inches.

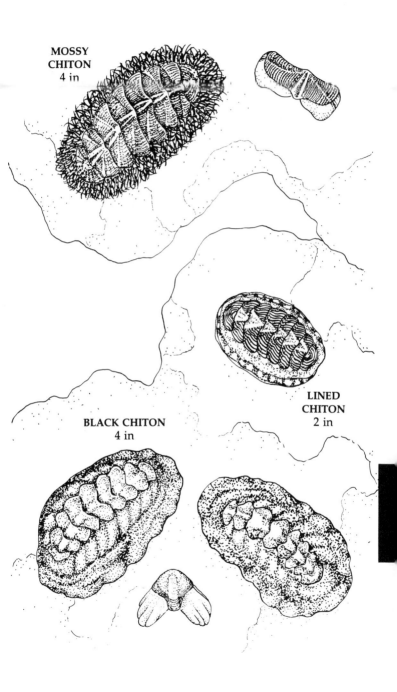

MOSSY CHITON 4 in

LINED CHITON 2 in

BLACK CHITON 4 in

■■■ Univalves
Class Gastropoda

Gastropods comprise the largest class of mollusks; over 80,000 species worldwide. Most have single, coiled shell (nudibranchs lack shell). Move by a wavelike rippling on muscular "foot." Most species have well-developed head with eyes and tentacles. Most have rasping tongue (radula) used by vegetarian snails for scraping algae off rocks and by predatory snails for drilling holes in barnacles or bivalves.

■■■ Keyhole Limpets
Family Fissurellidae

Told from "true limpets" by small opening in top of volcano-shaped shell, through which short siphon is visible.

■ KEYHOLE LIMPET
Diodora aspera

Volcano shape; hole on top. To about 2 inches. Feeds on encrusting sponges. Usually has a flesh-colored commensal scaleworm (*Arctinoe*) living under its mantle.

■■■ Abalones
Family Haliotidae

Large snaillike mollusk with thick, perforated shell. Harvested for food and pearly shell for millenia; eagerly sought by scuba divers. Also preyed on by octopus, crabs, and rockfishes. The animal, which can extend far beyond its shell, is fascinating to watch; can be viewed in the Seattle Aquarium.

■ NORTHERN (Pinto) ABALONE
Haliotis kamtschatkana

Disk-shaped, red-and-pink shell is rough outside, often covered by boring sponges or other organisms; inside it is pearly and iridescent. Most recent hole at edge of shell is used for water exchange. To 5 inches and may live 50 years. Found tightly clamped to rocks during day; grazes at night. Can move rather quickly on muscular foot, occasionally rearing up to trap a piece of kelp. Sometimes found intertidally. Subtidally, it is joined by the similar-sized **Northern Green Abalone** (*Haliotis walallensis*).

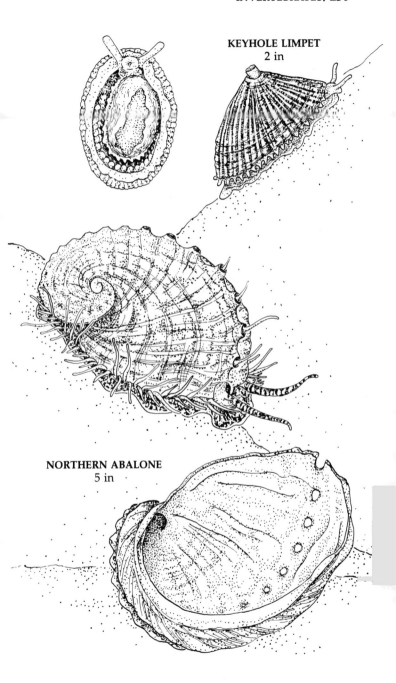

KEYHOLE LIMPET
2 in

NORTHERN ABALONE
5 in

■ Limpets
Families Lottidae and Acmaeidae

Familiar beach animals, usually found clinging tightly to rocks. Many local species; some vary in shape and may be difficult to tell apart. All have hard rasping teeth on a ribbon (radula) that works like sandpaper to scrape food off rocks. When submerged, many wander off to feed (often at night), later returning to same spot.

■ FINGER LIMPET
Lottia (Collisella) digitalis

Usually has a strongly ribbed and somewhat misshapen shell. Edge of shell is wavy and fluted; apex sometimes points forward rather than being at center of shell. Seen from above, shape is elliptical, narrower at one end than the other. To about 1 inch. Usually found high up on rocky beaches or on top of rocks in protected bays.

A similar limpet, *Lottia paradigitalis*, is usually smoother and flatter shelled. Less than 1 inch.

■ SHIELD LIMPET
Lottia (Collisella) pelta

Shell is slightly oval; sometimes ribbed, sometimes smooth; but apex is usually more pointed and centered than the other two *Lottia* species. Interior of shell is white to blue. To slightly over 1 inch.

■ MASKED LIMPET
Tectura (Notoacmea) persona

Found with Finger Limpet in the upper tidal zone of rocky shore or on exposed rocks of protected bays; usually clings to underside of rock or wave-washed rock crevice. Seen from above, shape is elliptical, often narrower at one end than the other. Seen from side, shell is fairly rounded; smooth on top and lightly ribbed near the edges. From below has facelike pattern. To 1½ inches.

■ PLATE LIMPET
Tectura (Notoacmea) scutum

Smooth, flattened shell; usually marked with interesting patterns of brown and white radiating from the low apex. Relatively large limpet, reaching 2 inches. Found on rocky beaches from low to high tide levels.

■ WHITECAP LIMPET
Acmaea mitra

Tall, conical shell (up to 1 inch tall, about the same as diameter of round base). Shell is dull white; often covered with algae, especially the pink encrusting corallines on which it feeds.

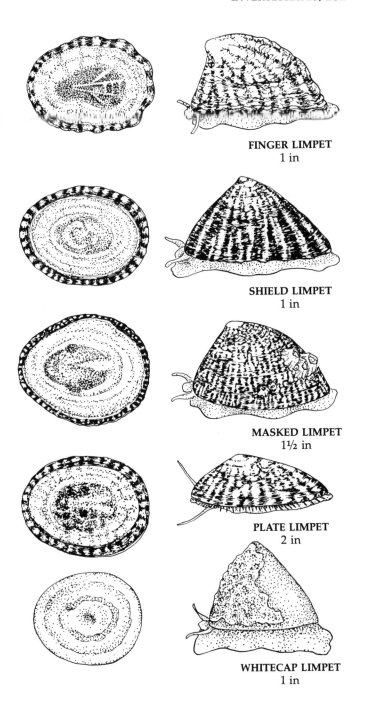

FINGER LIMPET
1 in

SHIELD LIMPET
1 in

MASKED LIMPET
1½ in

PLATE LIMPET
2 in

WHITECAP LIMPET
1 in

■ Snails   *Class* Gastropoda   (*Subclass* Prosobranchia)

Familiar univalve mollusks; all but a few species have coiled shells. Most shelled snails have, attached to the foot, a chitinous or shelly flap (operculum), which acts as trapdoor to tightly cover opening when snail withdraws; helps protect snail from predators and keeps intertidal species from drying out. Most have well-developed heads with eyes and tentacles. About half are vegetarians, half predatory; some scavenging or even parasitic.

■ Tritons   *Family* Cymatiidae

■ HAIRY TRITON   *Fusitriton oregonensis*

White shell is covered by bristly, grayish brown "periostracum." Inside of shell is pearly white. Graceful, pointed shell has 6 or so ribbed whorls; surprisingly light but very strong. To 5 inches; our largest snail after Moon Snail.

Mostly subtidal, but often seen during very low tides. Feeds on a variety of marine animals, including sea urchins. For much of the year seen paired; males ride on females and defend against other encroaching males. Females brood and protect egg masses, which resemble clusters of corn kernels.

■ Moon Snails   *Family* Naticidae

■ MOON SNAIL   *Polinices lewisii*

Globular shell is gray and smooth. The massive body, when extended, almost covers the shell but can withdraw completely when theatened. Our largest local snail; to 5 inches tall and equally broad.

Common in shallow subtidal areas on mud or sand substrate, where it works its way under the surface to feed on clams. Leaves a characteristic hole near hinge of prey's shell. During spring/summer breeding season it crawls up on sandbars and muddy sand beaches to lay eggs. Eggs are enclosed in familiar, rubbery "sand collars" formed around the extended mantle.

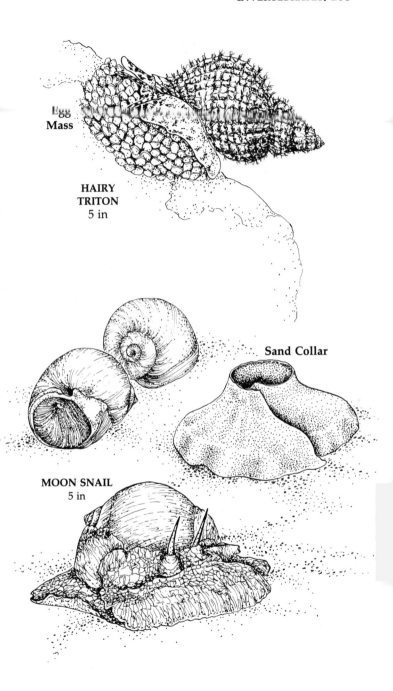

Egg
Mass

**HAIRY
TRITON**
5 in

Sand Collar

MOON SNAIL
5 in

■Periwinkles
Family Littorinidae

Strictly high intertidal. Can survive long periods out of water and are thought to be ancestors of most land snails. Like land snails, they exude slime to help in gliding over rough surfaces. Periwinkles have fat shells with rounded openings. Good eyes and large tentacles. Sexes separate; male has large penis to the right of head. Use long radula, with up to 300 rows of minute teeth, to scrape microscopic algae off rocks.

■SITKA PERIWINKLE
Littorina sitkana

Common on seaweed-covered upper intertidal rocks. Also seen in salt marshes. Round, grayish shell has turbanlike spire, which may be lighter colored. About 12 raised bands spiral up the shell, crossed by growth rings; but often the bands are worn down. To 8/10 inch.

■CHECKERED PERIWINKLE
Littorina scutulata

Smaller (to 6/10 inch) and more slender than the Sitka Periwinkle; more pointed at the top. Body whorl (lower portion) is dark and checkered with white spots. Like the Sitka, it is found on seaweed-covered intertidal rocks; but less likely to be seen in salt marshes.

■Top Shells
Family Trochidae

■TOP SHELL
Calliostoma ligatum

Almost triangular in cross section and pointed like a toy top. Shell circled by thin, cordlike ribs. Ribs are tan or white; furrows between are pink (the color of the encrusting red algae on which it is often found). Sometimes found intertidally but more abundant on rocks in shallow subtidal. Grazes on low-growing sessile animals and algal scum. To about 1 inch.

The **Ringed Top Shell** (*Calliostoma annulatum*) is even more colorful, violet and lime green. It is primarily an outer coast species but is found subtidally around the San Juan and Canadian Gulf islands.

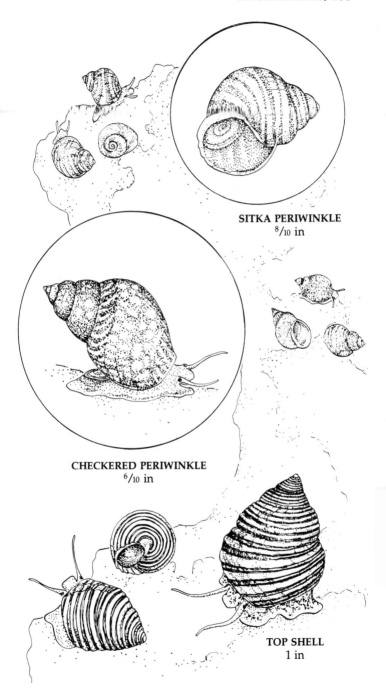

SITKA PERIWINKLE
8/10 in

CHECKERED PERIWINKLE
6/10 in

TOP SHELL
1 in

■Whelks
Family Murcidae

Important predators on mussels and barnacles, especially on the Acorn Barnacle. They drill a hole between the plates of the barnacle, insert digestive juices, and suck out the contents. Empty whelk shells, in turn, are used by hermit crabs. Egg masses resemble oat kernels.

■PURPLE WHELK
Nucella (Thais) lamellosa

Relatively large, heavy-bodied snail. Usually covered with frilly ridges and spiny cords (specimens on exposed rocks may be smooth). Opening (aperture) is narrow with a long canal at the base; spire is pointed. To over 2 inches.

■CHANNELED WHELK
Nucella (Thais) canaliculata

Slightly smaller than Purple Whelk. Its shell is distinctly and evenly ridged with about a dozen cords; the canal at the base of the aperture is almost closed.

■ROCK WHELK
Nucella (Thais) emarginata

Smallest of the 3 common whelks (to 1 inch). Its body ridges alternate between thick and thin.

■LEAFY HORNMOUTH
Ceratostoma foliatum

Distinctive snail found on rocks in areas of strong current. Outlandish shell has 3 leafy wings extending along the body, especially near opening (aperture). At base of aperture is toothlike "horn" and a tubular extension, upturned at the end, through which the snail extends its long siphon. To 3 inches. Feeds by drilling into barnacles and mussels.

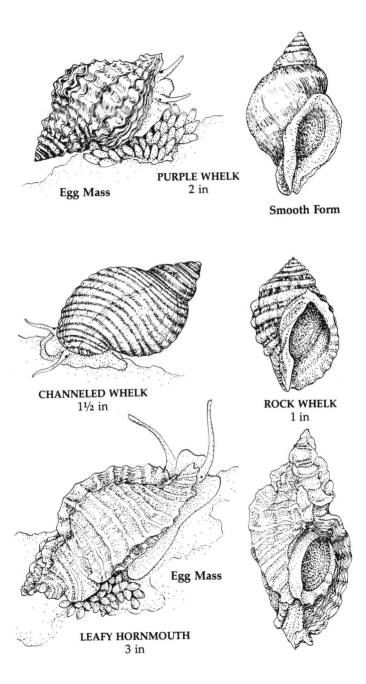

Egg Mass

PURPLE WHELK
2 in

Smooth Form

CHANNELED WHELK
1½ in

ROCK WHELK
1 in

Egg Mass

LEAFY HORNMOUTH
3 in

■■■Small Whelks
Family Buccinidae

■ SPINDLE SHELL (Dire Whelk)
Searlesia dira

Graceful, pointed shell is spiraled with numerous fine spiral cords crossed by broad, low ribs on the upper whorls and growth lines on the lower, or body whorl. Outer edge of opening (aperture) is finely toothed. Gray to brown. To 1½ inches.

Found on rocky shores in lower intertidal and shallow subtidal zones. Preys on periwinkles and other mollusks, barnacles, and worms. Shell is popular home for hermit crabs.

■■■Horn Shells
Family Potamididae

■ SCREW SHELL
Batillaria zonalis

Slender, graceful, pointed spire. Grayish cords have numerous brown beads. Much larger than similar Horn Shell; to 1½ inches. Found in great numbers on exposed mud flats of quiet bays. Feeds on surface diatoms. Exotic; native to Japan.

■■■Ceriths
Family Cerithiidae

■ HORN SHELL
Bittium eschrichtii

Small but distinctive. Long, slender straight-sided spire tapers to sharp point; 4 to 5 ridges coil along the 6 to 8 whorls. Usually found under rocks but sometimes seen in large numbers in shallows, especially near Eelgrass. Less than 1 inch.

■■■Dove Shells
Family Columbellidae

■ WRINKLED AMPHISSA
Amphissa columbiana

Sharply pointed spire. Body whorls are rounded and strongly ribbed; the ribs are crossed with numerous fine ridges, giving the shell a wrinkled or beaded appearance. The canal at base of opening (aperture) is almost closed; through it the snail extends its long siphon. To about 1 inch. A scavenger found on rocky and cobble beaches.

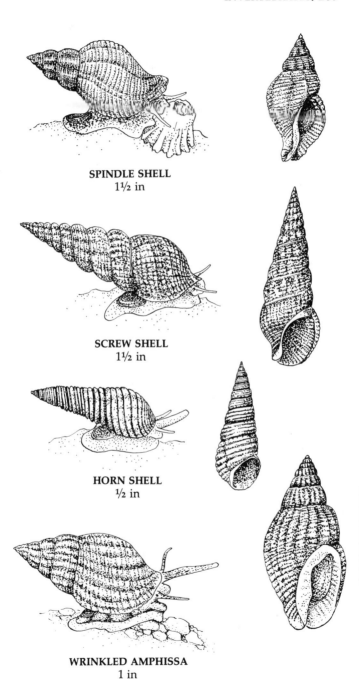

SPINDLE SHELL
1½ in

SCREW SHELL
1½ in

HORN SHELL
½ in

WRINKLED AMPHISSA
1 in

■ Nudibranchs (Sea slugs)

Order Nudibranchia
(*Subclass* Opisthobranchia)

Colorful shell-less gastropod mollusks. Most groups lack gills; instead take oxygen through body surface. To increase surface many species have developed bizarre outgrowths from dorsal surface (cerata). Most species have organs of smell (rhinophores) of various shapes on head area; some have second pair of tentacles. Most are hermaphrodites. Lay many ribbonlike egg clusters.

■ Dorid nudibranchs

(*Suborder* Doridacea)

Tend to be oval shaped and flattened. Stubby rhinophores noticeable near head. Cerata are clustered in flowery, retractable "branchial plume" around anus (toward rear of dorsal surface).

■ SEA LEMON

Archidoris montereyensis

Oval from top view; plump in middle and thin at edges. Pale to deep, dingy yellow with brown spots scattered over back. Pointed rhinophores up front; 6-part branchial plume at rear end. To 2 inches. Seen at low tide levels on rocky or cobble beaches. Eats encrusting sponges.

Another Sea Lemon, *Anisodoris nobilis,* is at least twice the size of *Archidoris*. It often shows more orange and has smaller spots; lacks spots on rhinophores.

■ RINGED DORIS

Diaulula (Discodoris) sandiegensis

Oval shape. Body is creamy white to gray, with various-size, dark brown, round spots or circles on back. Covered with tiny, stiff hairlike projections. Antennae are comblike. Feeds on encrusting sponges, especially Haliclona. To 3 inches.

■ ROUGH-MANTLED DORIS

Onchidoris bilamellata

Dark brown, cream, or orange. Dorsal side is bordered (mantled) with rough knobs; center is fairly smooth. Retractable bushy gills around anus number 16 to 32 in two semicircles. To 1 inch. Found on rocks and pilings in the shallow subtidal zone. Common intertidally winter and spring. Feeds on Acorn Barnacles.

■ RED NUDIBRANCH

Rostanga pulchra

Small red to orange body is well camouflaged against red or orange sponges (*Ophlitaspongia* and others) on which it feeds. Lays coils of red-orange egg masses on the same sponges. Front end is somewhat squared off. Two tubular, fringed rhinophores. Rear end more pointed; a fringed circle of anal gills. Found on rocks from lower intertidal to shallow subtidal. Usually less than 1 inch long.

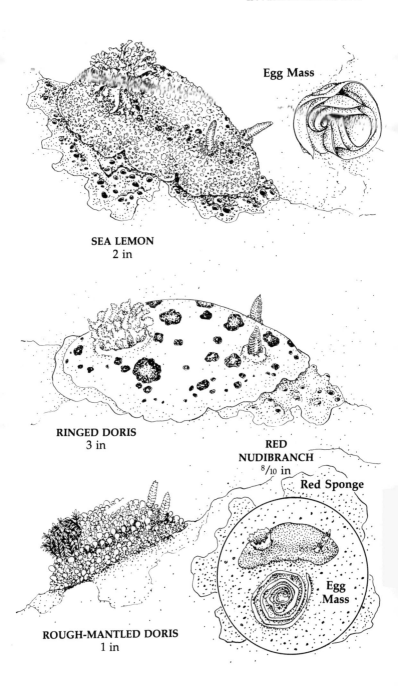

Egg Mass

SEA LEMON
2 in

RINGED DORIS
3 in

**RED
NUDIBRANCH**
8/10 in

Red Sponge

**Egg
Mass**

ROUGH-MANTLED DORIS
1 in

■Aeolid nudibranchs

(Suborder Aolidacea)

Tend to be cylindrical in basic body shape but body is often obscured by many large cerata, which grow from the entire dorsal surface. Darker digestive glands can often be seen ascending into translucent cerata.

■OPALESCENT NUDIBRANCH

Hermissenda (Phidiana) crassicornis

Body is translucent white. Slender, pointed cerata are tipped with orange; the brown lines that run up the middle of the cerata are digestive glands. Two white rhinophores extend from the head. To 2 inches. Found on floats and rocky beaches; more common subtidally, on rocks or sandy shell bottom, especially in Eelgrass. Omnivorous.

■SEA MOUSE

Aeolidea papillosa

White, tinged with pink, green, or brown. Many small branchial outgrowths from its flat, wide body give it a shaggy appearance. Two tentaclelike rhinophores project from bald patch on head end. To 2½ inches. Found in same habitats as Opalescent Nudibranch. Feeds on tentacles of sea anemones.

■CLOWN (Orange Tipped) NUDIBRANCH

Triopha catalinae

One of the most colorful of our nudibranchs. Cylindrical white or grayish body is spotted with bright orange, as are tips of rhinophores, antennae, and ring of feathery gills. Bright tips may advertise noxious substance to fish. To 2½ inches. Found among seaweeds on intertidal rocky beaches down to midsubtidal zone. Feeds on byozoans.

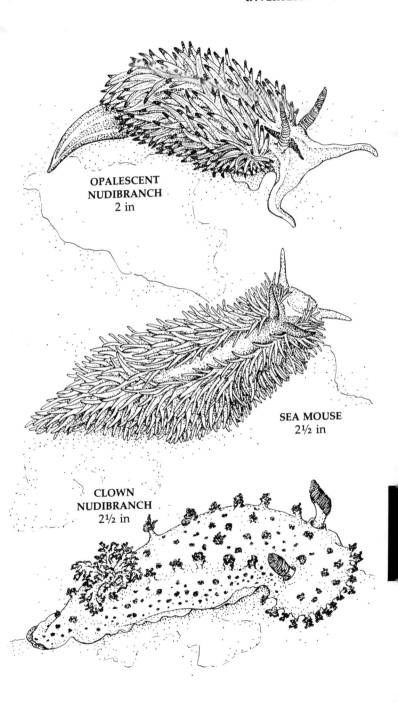

**OPALESCENT
NUDIBRANCH**
2 in

SEA MOUSE
2½ in

**CLOWN
NUDIBRANCH**
2½ in

▰Dendronotid nudibranchs   (*Suborder* Dendronotacea)

Basically cylindrical bodies. Cerata tend to be fewer than in the Aeolids but are often spectacularly branched or plumed.

▰HOODED NUDIBRANCH   *Melibe leonina*

Most bizarre of our sea slugs. It has a large, inflated "oral hood." A fringe of stiff hairs point in toward the center of the hood, helping it to trap tiny amphipods and other small crustaceans. The hood also closes to trap air, helping the nudibranch drift from place to place. There are 4 to 6 pairs of large dorsal cerata; digestive branches visible within. The bluish, almost transparent body reaches 4 inches. Usually found on Eelgrass.

▰Arminacean nudibranchs   (*Suborder* Arminacea)
▰BROWN-STRIPED NUDIBRANCH   *Armina californica*

Leaf-shaped body with thin brown and white stripes. Lacks dorsal cerata. Instead, has flaplike gills in a groove along the sides, between the foot and the overhanging dorsal skin. Two small divergent rhinophores at the "stem" side. Found in beds of Sea Pens, on which it feeds. To 3 inches.

▰FROSTED NUDIBRANCH   *Dirona albolineata*

Translucent; white to varied pastels. Wide, triangular cerata are sharply pointed and edged with white. To over 2 inches. Mostly subtidal. Feeds on small snails (which it cracks with its teeth) and other small organisms.

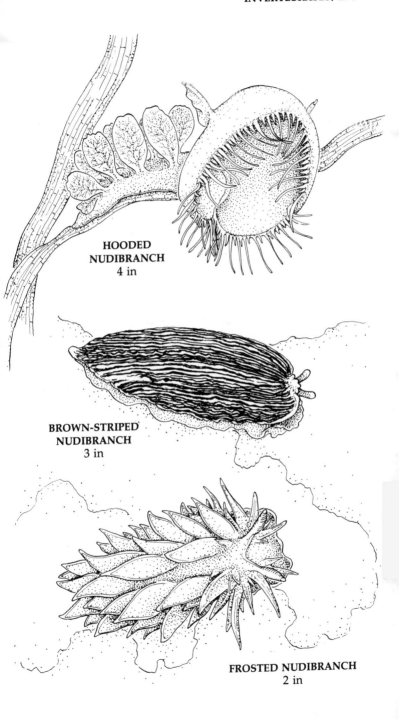

HOODED NUDIBRANCH
4 in

BROWN-STRIPED NUDIBRANCH
3 in

FROSTED NUDIBRANCH
2 in

■■ Bivalves

Class Bivalva

Soft parts covered by two hinged, calcified shells (valves). When disturbed or exposed to air, valves are closed tightly by 1 or 2 large adductor muscles. Second largest mollusk class, next to gastropods (snails). Most have siphons to draw in water to be filtered for food and oxygen.

■■ Mussels

Family Mytilidae

Strong, thin, pear-shaped shells. Filter-feeders. Attach to rocks by strong "byssal threads"; sometimes clump together in great numbers.

■ BLUE MUSSEL

Mytilus edulus

Common intertidal mussel of protected waters. Adult shell is bluish black outside (juvenile's is brown). Interior is pearly; purple around edges. Brownish byssal threads. Grows to 2½ inches. Clumps on rocks and pilings. Feeds on plankton filtered from the water; preyed on by *Pisaster* and other sea stars and *Nucella* whelks. A productive aquaculture crop in Europe; raised by raft culture locally.

■ CALIFORNIA MUSSEL

Mytilus californianus

Tends to be larger than the Blue Mussel (to 8 inches); shell more inflated and rougher, with radial ribs and coarse growth lines. Prefers strong wave action; found locally only on exposed rocks in San Juan and Canadian Gulf islands.

■ HORSE MUSSEL

Modiolus modiolus

Young specimen is brown and covered with long, fuzzy hairs; adult resembles Blue Mussel but grows to 6 inches. Found on rocks and shelly mud in quiet bays; tends to be subtidal; abundant in very deep water.

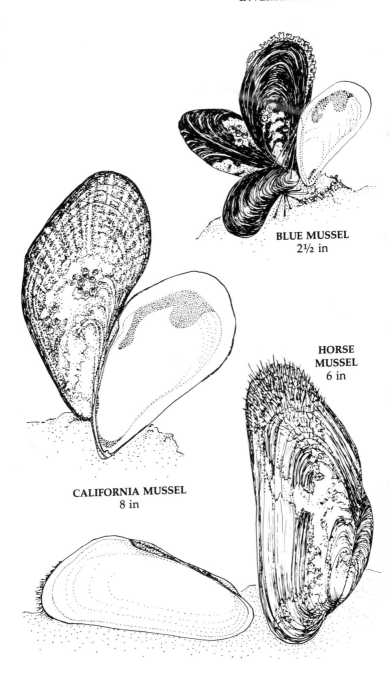

BLUE MUSSEL
2½ in

HORSE
MUSSEL
6 in

CALIFORNIA MUSSEL
8 in

■ Scallops
Family Pectinidae

Large and diverse group of swimming bivalves. Small, light-sensitive eyes (visible when valves are open) line the mantle below edge of shell valves. Valves are connected by ball-and-socket hinge; closed by a single, large adductor muscle (the part we eat).

■ PINK SCALLOP
Chlamys hastata

One "wing" or "ear" much larger than other. Upper valve has ribs radiating from hinge (alternate ones more prominent); ribs have small spines. Upper valve is pinkish but usually covered by a layer of sponge. To more than 2 inches.

Often attaches by byssal threads to subtidal rock but can swim freely (especially when threatened by predatory sea stars) by clapping its valves to expel water. Lacks siphon; filters plankton from water taken in between gaping valves. Mostly subtidal in Puget Sound; sought by divers.

The **Smooth Pectin** (*Chlamys rubida*) looks much like the Pink Scallop, but its ribs lack spines. Right valve has ruffly ribs; left valve is smooth. Subtidal; found with the Pink Scallop on gravel and shell.

■ PURPLE HINGED ROCK SCALLOP
Hinnites giganteus

Similar to Pink Scallop when young; swims freely. Later attaches to rock; upper valve grows thick and misshapen with many beaded ridges. Often covered with boring sponges, encrusting algae, or other encrusting organisms. Even when young can be told by deep purple color inside hinge. Grows to 6 inches. Mostly subtidal but attaches to intertidal rocks in exposed areas.

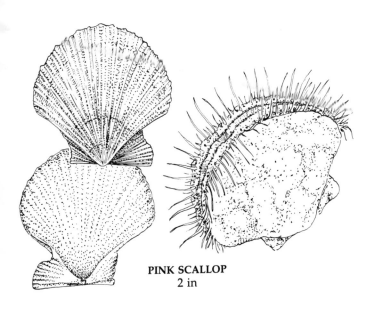

PINK SCALLOP
2 in

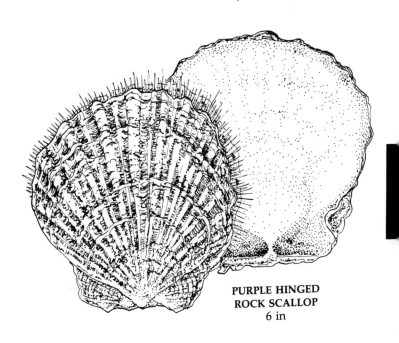

**PURPLE HINGED
ROCK SCALLOP**
6 in

■ Jingle Shells

Family Anomiidae

■ ROCK OYSTER (Jingle Shell)

Podods...es cepio

Roundish in top view. Thin lower valve is flat but conforms to curve of rock face; attaches by byssal through through hole in shell. When found washed up on beach, these lower valves are called "jingle shells." Upper valve is thicker and more curved. To 5 inches or more. When the upper valve is elevated for feeding, the bright red-orange flesh inside can be seen.

■ Oysters

Family Ostreidae

Common bivalve mollusks highly prized as food. Eight North American species, 2 local. Individuals usually male or female but sex reversal is common. Eggs produced in spring or summer; develop inside mantle cavity. Mature oyster can produce 500,000 larvae each year. Larvae swim around for a few weeks before settling; crawl around to find good spot and cement themselves to hard substrate (often other oyster shells).

Filter feeders. Preyed on by sea stars, crabs, and oyster drills. Pearls produced by edible oysters are of little value.

■ OLYMPIA OYSTER

Ostrea lurida

Small but tasty. Found in quiet bays in Puget Sound. Gray, gnarly, rounded valves are of equal size, rarely growing to more than 2 inches. Inside of shell is more colorful than Pacific Oyster's but without dash of purple.

Once an important commercial shellfish, especially in southern Puget Sound and Hood Canal. Labor costs, slow maturation (4 to 5 years), overharvesting, and water pollution led to sharp declines in the 1920s and 1930s; now largely supplanted by Pacific Oyster, though some are grown for luxury market.

■ PACIFIC OYSTER

Crassostrea gigas

Thick, fluted, misshapen shells; white or grayish. Lower valve curved; upper is flat and fits into lower. Inside of shell is white but stained purple around adductor muscle scar. To 10 inches.

Introduced from Japan early in century; naturalized locally. Valuable aquaculture crop. Since natural reproduction is spotty, most growers annually import tiny oysters (spat) on strings of empty oyster shells (cultch). Spread on beaches or strung from rafts; harvested in 2 to 4 years.

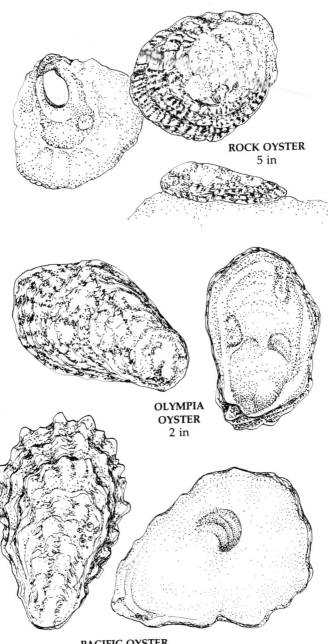

ROCK OYSTER
5 in

OLYMPIA OYSTER
2 in

PACIFIC OYSTER
10 in

■Cockles
Family Cardiidae

■HEART COCKLE
Clinocardium nuttallii

Inflated shell is thick but brittle; cracks easily when dropped from low heights by gulls. About ? dozen low ribs radiate from beaked hinge (umbo); ribs are crossed by growth rings; older specimens often worn smooth. Long, muscular foot; can "pole-vault" away from predatory sea stars. Paired siphons are very short; lives on or close to surface. Found on muddy sand beaches from midintertidal zone to 80-foot depth.

■Venus Clams
Family Veneridae

Large family includes quahogs, venuses, and littlenecks, our Butter Clam, and the Pismo clam of California beaches. All have 2 similar valves that are generally heart shaped and have a prominent, rounded beak (umbo) near hinge. Most have conspicuous concentric growth lines; some have thin ribs radiating from umbo.

■NATIVE LITTLENECK
(Steamer Clam)
Protothaca staminea

Shaped somewhat like Heart Cockle, but valves are thinner and more flattened; beak is smooth and pointed. Many fine ridges radiate from just below beak to edges of valves; ridges are crossed by light growth rings. Sometimes patterned with brown stains. Inner edge of one valve, opposite the umbo, is bumpy. Fused siphons are short, and so it lives just below the surface in muddy sand or gravel. Found in great numbers from midintertidal levels to about 60-foot depth; often with the deeper-burrowing Butter Clam. To 4 inches.

Native littlenecks grow and repopulate slowly; take 4 to 6 years to grow to a commercial size of 2 inches. May take 10 to 25 years for a bed to repopulate and mature.

■MANILA CLAM
(Japanese Littleneck)
Tapes philippinarum (japonica)

Valves more oblong than Native Littleneck's: more pointed at the narrow end and more squared at the broad end; ridges are more widely spaced. Lives near the surface on muddy sand or pea gravel beaches. Abundant in sheltered bays; high intertidal to shallow subtidal. To 4 inches.

Accidently introduced to Puget Sound in the 1920s in shipments of Pacific Oyster. Grows to commercial size in just 2 years; can tolerate crowded conditions and lives high up on the beach above the reach of most predators. Has become our most productive cultivated shellfish.

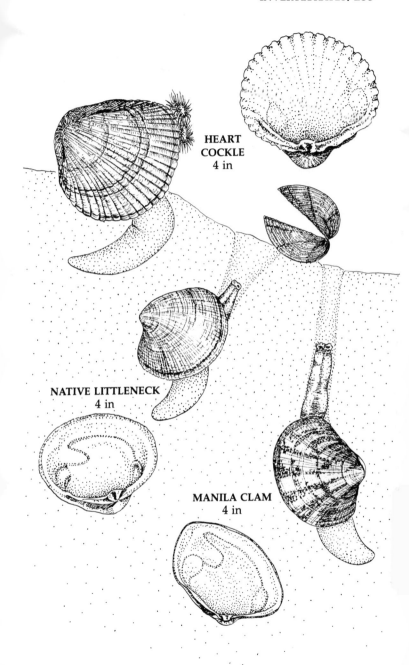

HEART COCKLE
4 in

NATIVE LITTLENECK
4 in

MANILA CLAM
4 in

■ BUTTER CLAM
Saxidomus giganteus

Large, thick-shelled clam. Yellowish when young; gray or white when mature, sometimes stained black by iron sulfate in the mud. Hinge is thick; valves fit together in a complex pattern of grooves and teeth. Valves closes tightly (unlike Horse Clam). Grows to 6 inches; reaches commercial size in 2 to 3 inches and repopulates quickly.

Found from low intertidal to 60-foot depth; in the same gravelly mud as the Native Littleneck, but deeper (8 to 14 inches) below surface.

■ Macoma Clams
Family Tellinidae

A large genus of northern clams. Two separate siphons.

■ BENT-NOSED CLAM
Macoma nasuta

Unusual shape: when viewed toward hinge, the narrow side of valves are bent at an angle. Lies on its side, 4 to 6 inches below surface; long, orange siphons reach surface from between the bent valves. Valves are white but partially covered by a flaky, brown covering (periostracum). A small clam; to 2 inches. Lives in mud of sheltered bays; from intertidal to 130-foot depth.

Macoma inquinata is about the same size and color as the bent-nosed clam, but valves are more inflated and are not bent. Siphons are not orange.

■ SAND CLAM
Macoma secta

Valves are white and fairly smooth. One valve flattened, the other more inflated; both have a sharp bend line along one edge. Uses its mobile incurrent siphon to suck detritus from surface of sand. To 4 inches. Lives 8 to 10 inches below surface of sandy beaches.

■ Soft-shell Clams
Family Myacidae

■ SOFT-SHELL CLAM
Mya arenaria

Thin valves crack easily. Elliptical, but more pointed at the siphon end. White to gray with broad, concentric growth rings. One valve is flatter and inside has a spoon-shaped shelf (chondrophore) extending from the hinge. Neck is long and leathery; does not fully retract. To 4 inches.

Introduced from the Atlantic Coast with oyster spat in the 1920s. Found in sandy mud from upper intertidal to 130-foot depth. Prefers areas of low salinity such as river mouths. Lives about 8 inches below the surface.

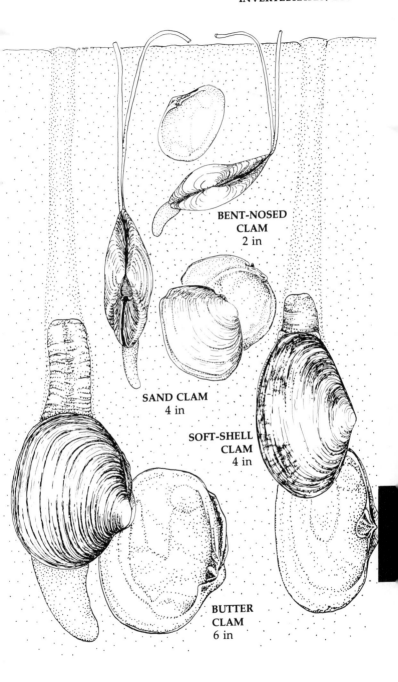

BENT-NOSED
CLAM
2 in

SAND CLAM
4 in

SOFT-SHELL
CLAM
4 in

BUTTER
CLAM
6 in

■Mactra Surf Clams

Family Mactridae

■HORSE (Gaper) CLAM

Iresus capax

Our largest intertidal clam (to 8 inches). Valves are chalky white edged with dark, thin, flaky covering (periostracum); sometimes blackened by sulfides in the mud. Valves gape apart around siphon, which cannot fully retract into shell. Tip of brown siphon covered by pair of large, fleshy flaps.

Found from just above low tide to 60-foot depth. Found 20 inches below surface in gravelly mud (to 12 inches deep in clay); often found with Butter Clams and Native Littlenecks. Squirts water forcefully (up to 2 feet high).

Often parasitized by tiny **Pea Crab** (*Pinnixa faba* or 2 other species), which lives in the clam's mantle.

■Geoducks

Family Hiatellidae

■GEODUCK

Panope abrupta (*Panopea generosa*)

Pronounced "gooeyduck." By far the largest clam locally, but mostly subtidal. Valves may reach 8 inches; neck to 3 feet long when extended, 10 inches contracted. Weighs up to 20 pounds. Valves gape at siphon end like those of Horse Clam but shape is more rectangular. No hard flaps on tip of siphon. Lives 2 to 3 feet below surface. Found from just below lowest tide to 200-foot depth.

Geoducks average 40 to 60 years old and can live 150 years. Harvested commercially by hard hat divers from subtidal beds leased from the state. Grows at rate of an inch per year; takes 6 to 7 years to grow to commercial size of over 20 pounds. Repopulation is slow, successful "sets" are periodic; may take 10 to 30 years for a bed to mature.

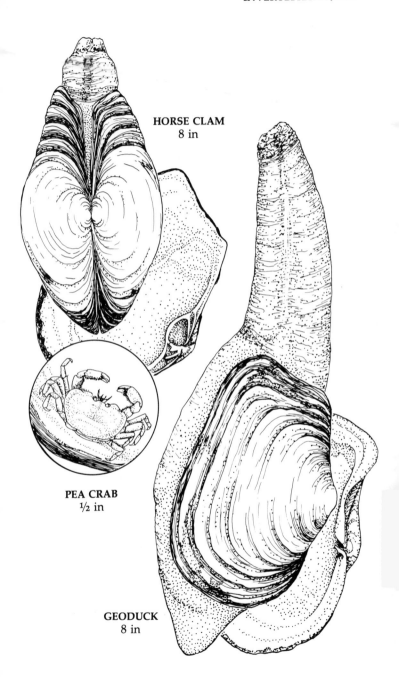

HORSE CLAM
8 in

PEA CRAB
½ in

GEODUCK
8 in

■ Piddocks

Family Pholadidae

■ ROUGH PIDDOCK

Zirfaea pilsbryii

Rough, filelike surface on lower half of shell. Uses muscular foot to rotate shell back and forth to bore a permanent burrow deep into hard clay or soft rock. Anterior half of each valve (foot end) is ridged with wavy concentric growth rings; posterior half (siphon end) is smooth and much like Butter Clam's. Both valve ends gape; neck and foot cannot be withdrawn. Shell grows to 4 inches; neck extends 4 inches farther, even when fully contracted. Neck is flesh colored and covered with tiny white bumps; tip branches into two separate round siphons, which are impressively large when open. Found from lowest tide zone to deep subtidal.

■ Shipworms

Family Teredinidae

■ SHIPWORM

Bankia setacea

Shipworms are not worms but odd clams. Long (to 3 feet), fleshy, wormlike body extends from small boring shell that has sharp "wings." Small but strong foot rotates the boring shell back and forth, somewhat like a Rough Piddock, boring a pencil-diameter tunnel through submerged wood. Timbers riddled with such tunnels can often collapse. Shipworm can digest some of the wood that it bores, but most of its nutrition seems to come from planktonic algae filtered from the water.

Arthropods

Phylum Arthropoda

Crustaceans

Class Crustacea

ustaceans are as numerous in the sea as their fellow arthropods,
insects, are on land. They have a hard external "exoskeleton" of
on, to which muscles are attached; the chiton is calcified in crus-
ns such as crabs. Moveable appendages (legs, mouthparts, and
nae) are segmented, the hard segments connected by softer ma-
at the joints.

crustaceans grow, the exoskeleton is periodically sloughed
a larger one grown. Many crab shells found on beaches are
ed exoskeltons of growing crabs. Hermit crabs, which protect
ft abdomens in abondoned snail shells, must find larger
they grow.

largest crustacean groups include amphipods, isopods, bar-
decapods (hermit crabs, true crabs, lobsters). Copepods,
s (krill), cladocerans, cumaceans, and ostracodes (along
od larvae and small amphipods) are found in tremendous
mong the open-water plankton; they are very important
s for larger crustaceans, small fish, the juveniles of larger
baleen whales.

des

Subclass Ostracoda

ic crustaceans. Unusual body appears to be covered by
shell (often transparent). Jointed legs, antennae, and
nd beyond the outer covering. Often found on sedi-
rs of barnacles or tube worms.

Copepods

Order Calanoida
(*Subclass* Copepoda)

pair of long antennae. Body narrows toward pos-
red or orange. Found in great numbers in the
important to the open-water (pelagic) food web.
d other single-celled algae. Often found with egg
ails.

Copepods

Order Harpacticoida
(*Subclass* Copepoda)

parent amphipods. Found on seaweeds or
ediments. Extremely important to juvenile
itus (decaying plant material).

Order Cumacea   (*Subclass* Malacostraca)
flexible posterior. Usually under ½ inch.
d mostly on detritus.

rder Mysidacea   (*Subclass* Malacostraca)
shrimp." Straight, slender bodies are al-
rk eyes. Usually seen in dense schools.

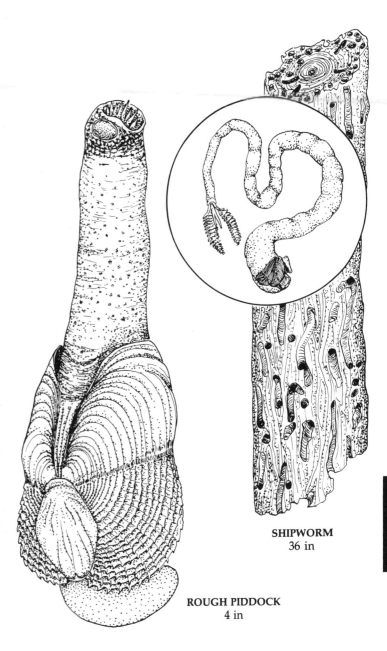

SHIPWORM
36 in

ROUGH PIDDOCK
4 in

Octopus and Squid
Class Cephalopoda

Most active and highly evolved class of mollusks. Eight or more arms surround the mouth, which in most groups has horny beak and radular teeth. Two gills, 2 kidneys, and 3 hearts. Eyes are particularly well-developed.

Octopuses have 8 arms (with rows of suction cups beneath); squids have 10 arms, of which 2 are specialized for breeding. Both capture prey with arms, bite with beaklike jaws. Both can squirt black fluid and can jet backwards with great speed. Some squid species form huge schools and are hunted by many species of fish, marine mammals, and seabirds; a major link in the ocean food web.

GIANT PACIFIC OCTOPUS
Octopus dofleini

World's largest octopus. In Alaskan waters male reportedly grows to arm spread of 32 feet. Local maximum about 20 feet (7 feet is more common). Female rarely reaches 6 feet because she dies at 3 years of age after brooding young. Skin is ridged by sharp folds. Has large pigmentation cells and can change color as response to background or circumstances.

Lives in caves and crevices; can squeeze through very small openings. After mating, female shuts herself in cave to care for strings of ricelike eggs, which hang from ceiling. She does not feed during this time and dies as eggs hatch (see McLachlin and Ayres for fascinating story of breeding). Hunts crabs; cracks shell with parrot-like beak. Preyed on by Wolf-eel, Lingcod, and scuba divers.

The **Red Octopus** (*Octopus rubescens*) is a much smaller species (to about 6 inches). Can be told from baby Giant Pacific Octopus by its lack of skin folds and by its rougher skin.

OPALESCENT SQUID
Loligo opalescens

Slender. Large eyes. Short arms. Long, sleek mantle has two triangular fins. Very fast swimmer; in schools. To about 6 inches. Returns to inland waters starting in October; spawns in January. Fished in Puget Sound from piers at night in late autumn.

STUBBY SQUID
Gonatus fabricii

About the same length as the Opalescent Squid (6 inches) but stockier; head and arms are darker; mantle is spotted. Both species feed on small fishes, shrimps, and other small crustaceans.

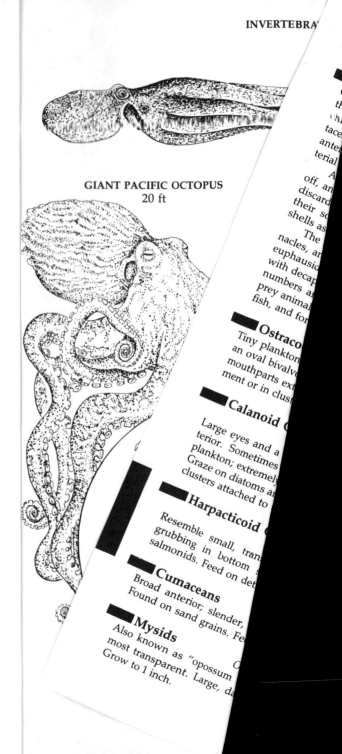

GIANT PACIFIC OCTOPUS
20 ft

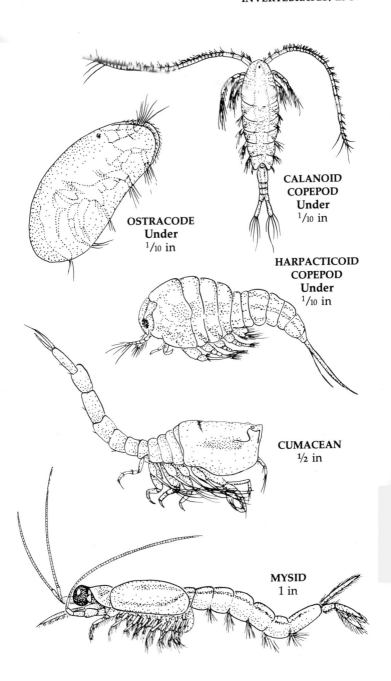

CALANOID
COPEPOD
Under
1/10 in

OSTRACODE
Under
1/10 in

HARPACTICOID
COPEPOD
Under
1/10 in

CUMACEAN
1/2 in

MYSID
1 in

Barnacles
Subclass Cirripedia

Barnacles have been described as shrimp standing on their heads. Planktonic larvae settle on rock, shell, or piece of wood and wander around until they find an open space; cement to substrate by their antennules; then undergo metamorphosis into the adult form. Adults protected by 6 rounded outer plates, and by 4 inner plates, which close up tightly when exposed to air. When the tide returns, the plates open. Modified legs sweep the current in rhythmic motion, collecting drifting detritus and plankton.

Three species are common intertidally. A few others may be seen occasionally. The beautiful **Giant Barnacle** (*Balanus nubilis*), which is intertidal on the open coast, is subtidal in Puget Sound; grows to 3 inches. The unusual **Goose Barnacle**, *Mitella (Pollicipes) polymerus*, is stalked and has only 5 outer plates; found on outer coast or exposed situations in San Juan and Canadian Gulf islands.

SMALL ACORN BARNACLE
Chthamalus dalli

Smallest of our common barnacles; grows to only about ⅓ inch. Found with larger Acorn Barnacle (*Balanus*) but can be told by the cross-shaped pattern made by the closed inner plates; usually darker than *Balanus* and can grow higher up on the beach. When *Chthamalus* and *Balanus* compete for space, *Balanus* pushes the smaller barnacle off the substrate.

ACORN BARNACLE
Balanus glandula

The most common barnacle from California to Alaska. Medium size; grows to about ½ inch tall and the same diameter. When densely crowded, grows in tall hexagonal columns.

Found on floats, pilings, rock, shell, kelp, and driftwood at upper tide levels, but below the highest individuals of the smaller, darker *Chthamalus dalli*. Notice the sharp curves in the line where the inner plates meet. A favorite food for sea stars (especially *Pisaster*, the Purple Sea Star) and sea snails (especially *Nucella* whelks).

THATCHED BARNACLE
Semibalanus cariosus

Largest of our 3 common intertidal barnacles; grows to 2 inches diameter; taller than wide. Outer plates are usually "thatched" with ropey lines down sides. Densely crowded ones grow as tall columns and are smoother; in this condition, they are hard to tell from *Balanus* (previous species), but are usually larger, darker, and found at lower beach levels. Inner plates meet in a wavy line, somewhat like that of *Balanus*. The dominant barnacle at lower tide levels, their lower limit often determined by the voracious Purple Sea Star.

**SMALL ACORN
BARNACLE**
$3/10$ in

ACORN BARNACLE
$1/2$ in

**THATCHED
BARNACLE**
2 in

▰▰Isopods   *Order* Isopoda   (*Subclass* Malacostraca)

Order includes the familiar terrestrial "pill bugs" found in garden and forest litter. Many marine species are parasitic on larger crustaceans or fishes. Can be told from other common beach crustaceans by wide, flattened bodies and seven similar pairs of tiny legs. The "gribble" (*Limnoria lignorum*)—not illustrated—is a small but important marine isopod; it burrows into wood like a terrestrial termite, reducing it to a spongy mass.

▪ROCKWEED ISOPOD   *Idotea wosnesenskii*

A relatively large isopod (to 1½ inches). Last segment behind final set of legs (telson) is large and flattened, tipped with a small point. Generally a smooth olive-green; but a color phase that lives on pink encrusting coralline algae is colorfully camouflaged in pinks, white, and brown. Found under cobble, under rocks at the edges of tide pools, in seaweed attached to floats, and on Eelgrass. Feeds on algal detritus.

▪EELGRASS ISOPOD   *Idotea resecata*

About the same color and width as the Eelgrass on which it is found and to which it tightly clings. Last segment behind final set of legs (telson) is concave and resembles a cut blade of eelgrass. Grows to about 1½ inches.

▪OREGON PILL BUG   *Gnorimosphaeroma oregonense*

Smaller and less flattened than *Idotea* species; usually less than half an inch long. Drab and grayish. Rolls up into a ball (like the terrestrial pill bug) when disturbed. Found in large assemblies among barnacles and mussels in the same habitats as the Rockweed Isopod, but prefers less salty water.

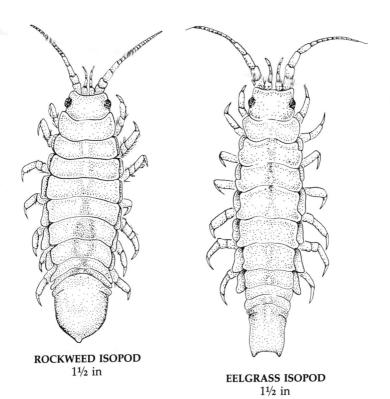

ROCKWEED ISOPOD
1½ in

EELGRASS ISOPOD
1½ in

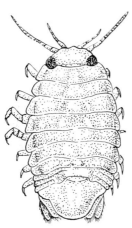

OREGON PILL BUG
½ in

Amphipods   *Order* Amphipoda   (*Subclass* Malacostraca)

Flattened laterally (side-to-side). Appendages on last 3 abdominal segments give appearance of ten pairs of legs. Many small species can be found darting around tide pools and crawling under seaweeds. Feed mostly on seaweeds and detritus.

AMPHITHOE   *Amphithoe* sp.

A genus of relatively large amphipods (to a little over 1 inch) found among the seaweeds growing on floats.

COROPHIUM   *Corophium* sp.

Body is not flattened side-to-side. Second pair of antennae are stout. A small amphipod (under ½ inch), which forms soft tubes in masses of detritus, on which it feeds.

BEACH HOPPER (Sand Flea)   *Traskorchestia traskiana*

Small (under 1 inch); drab gray-green. Hops around like flea in perpetual motion on wrack of seaweeds left stranded by tide on upper levels of beach. As the seaweed dries out, beach hoppers retreat into the moist center of the pile or dig into the sand. If you disturb the wrack, hundreds of beach hoppers will usually jump out. An important food for sanderlings and other migrating shorebirds.

A larger beach hopper, ***Megalorchestia californiana***, is found on beaches of outer coast. Pinkish, with long reddish orange antennae.

SKELETON SHRIMP   *Caprella* spp.

Strange-looking amphipods. Abdomen is so slender that the creature seems to be all antennae and legs, thus the common name. Looks like small praying mantis because of long, grasping first and second legs, which are widely separated. Last segment consists of a hooklike appendage, used for anchoring the flexible animal onto seaweeds or Eelgrass while it feeds on diatoms and detritus. Found in large numbers in Eelgrass beds, or at the edge of the water on sandy and muddy beaches.

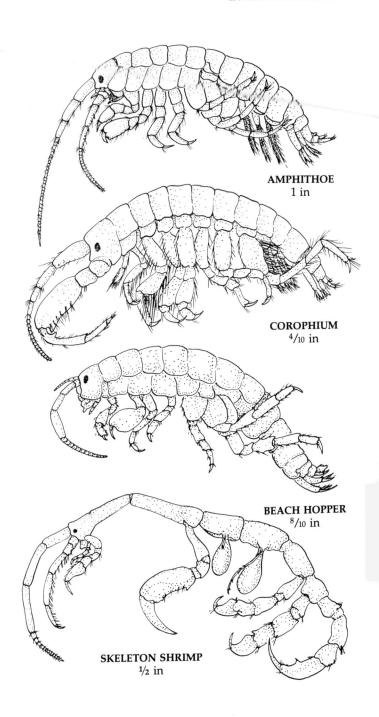

AMPHITHOE
1 in

COROPHIUM
⁴/₁₀ in

BEACH HOPPER
⁸/₁₀ in

SKELETON SHRIMP
½ in

▰Swimming Shrimps ("Natantia")

Order Decapoda (part)

■BROKEN-BACK SHRIMP

Heptacarpus spp.

Shrimps of this genus are commonly found under and around sea-weeds in tide pools. Translucent; color depends on the local sea-weed. Grows to about 1 inch. The name "broken-back" comes from the sharp bend in the abdomen behind the legs. Darts backward by flexing tail (last segments) forward. Feeds on tiny copepods and amphipods.

■COON-STRIPE SHRIMP

Pandalus danae

Brightly colored; red, brown and white stripes. Long antennae. Rostrum is upturned and spiny. To about 5 inches. Abundant around docks or submerged logs, especially at night. Feeds on zooplankton and small crustaceans.

▰Crawling Shrimps, Hermit Crabs, Crabs ("Reptantia")

Order Decapoda (part)

■GHOST (SAND) SHRIMP

Callianassa californiensis

A husky but delicate shrimp. Its exoskeleton is orange-pink to trans-lucent and quite soft. Grows to 4 inches; reportedly lives to 10 years.

Burrows in sand or mud, throwing up a hill around the 2 or more openings to its U-shaped tunnel (these hills can be seen in great numbers on muddy tideflats). Feeds on detritus and bacteria gleaned from the mud it processes. Fans water through its burrow, which may be inhabited by other, smaller organisms. Two species of para-sitic copepods are commonly seen beneath the ghost shrimp's trans-lucent exterior.

■MUD SHRIMP

Upogebia pugettensis

A large, burrowing shrimp; somewhat stockier than the similar-sized Ghost Shrimp (to 4 inches). Its exterior is bluish gray and noticeably fringed on the head, abdomen, and appendages. Prefers muddier beaches than the Ghost Shrimp, but the two species are of-ten found together. Does not build a hill around its tunnel entrance. Feeds on detritus. Parasitized by isopods and copepods and more commonly by a small commensal clam (***Orobitella rugifera***), which at-taches under the base of the mud shrimp's tail.

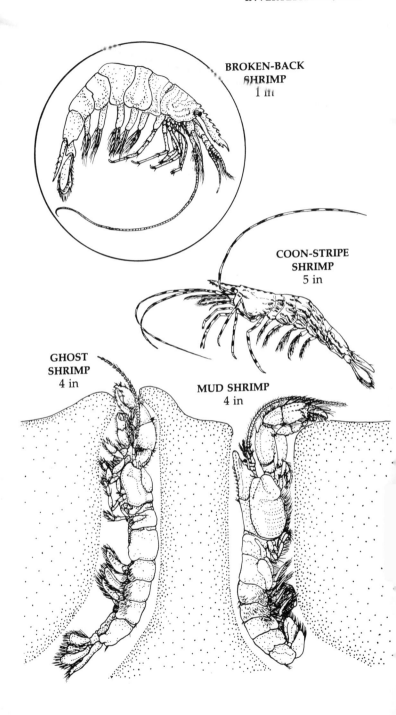

**BROKEN-BACK
SHRIMP**
1 in

**COON-STRIPE
SHRIMP**
5 in

**GHOST
SHRIMP**
4 in

MUD SHRIMP
4 in

■ Hermit Crabs
Family Paguridae

Hermit crabs' soft abdomens are narrow and curled to fit into a snail shell; they move to progressively larger shells as they grow. Long antennae; eyes on mobile stalks. Pugnacious, especially when looking for a larger shell. Feed on algae and/or detritus, and scavenge bits of animal matter. Sometimes seen in great breeding masses.

Three species are intertidal. Of the 17 or so subtidal species, 1 lives in empty tube worm tubes, 3 others sometimes live in hard sponges.

■ HAIRY HERMIT CRAB
Pagurus hirsutiusculus

Legs and antennae are noticeably hairy. Legs and claws are spotted white; legs 2 and 3 have narrow blue or white bands. Antennae are green with white spots. The most common hermit crab in upper tide pools. Often chooses shells that appear too small for it and cannot withdraw completely; yet the small shell allows this species to be highly mobile. Quickly abandons shell when picked up.

■ GRANULAR HERMIT CRAB
Pagurus granosimanus

About the same size as the Hairy Hermit Crab but relatively hairless and lacks white spots on antennae. Usually found at lower tide levels. It can withdraw entirely within its shell.

■ Porcelain Crabs
Family Porcellanidae

Not "true crabs"; more closely related to hermit crabs.

■ PORCELAIN CRAB
Petrolisthes eriomerus

Round body and broad, relatively massive claws are flattened. Bluish gray to reddish brown. Grows to about 2 inches (including claws). Usually found hiding under rocks. When picked up, easily sheds legs or claws, which grow back quickly.

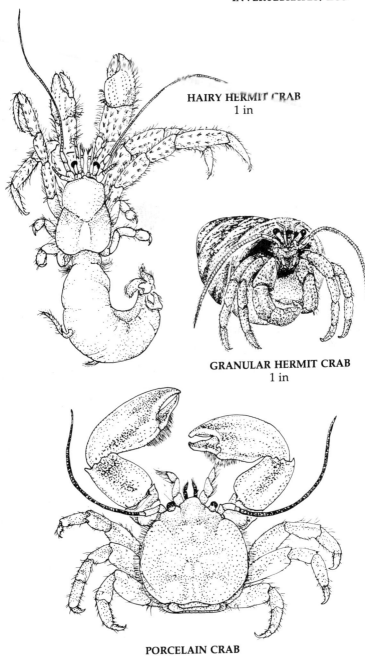

HAIRY HERMIT CRAB
1 in

GRANULAR HERMIT CRAB
1 in

PORCELAIN CRAB
2 in

■ "True Crabs"
Section Brachyura

Large, familiar crustaceans. Five pairs of walking legs, one pair modified as grasping claws. Head and thorax are covered by a single hard "carapace." Abdomen is small, curls under carapace. Eyes are often on mobile stalks; antennae usually are small.

■ GREEN SHORE CRAB
Hemigrapsus oregonensis

A small, active crab. Grayish green, often flecked with black; claws are whitish. Edges of carapace fringed with whitish hairs. To 2 inches. Hides under rocks on cobble beaches; often seen in great numbers in shallows (especially in sandy or estuarine habitats). In salt marshes it burrows into the mud. Feeds mostly on Sea Lettuce and other green algae.

■ PURPLE SHORE
(Purple Rock) CRAB
Hemigrapsus nudus

Similar in size to Green Shore Crab (up to 2 inches). Adult is dark red; claws pinkish with dark red spots. Hairless. Juvenile is lighter, varicolored; often whitish with dark claw tips. Carapace is straighter sided than Green Shore Crab's. Often seen with Green Shore Crab but more common in rocky habitats; both burrow into mud in salt marshes. Feeds mostly on Sea Lettuce and other green algae.

■ BLACK-CLAWED CRAB
Lophopanopeus bellus

A small (to 1 inch) crab found with the Porcelain Crab and the Green and Purple shore crabs under rocks at the lower levels of cobble beaches. Like the larger Red Rock and Oregon Rock crabs, its claws are tipped with black, but the color of the carapace is drab, the claws are broad and flat, and the undersides of the claws are light. Two sets of 3 broad spines on the front edge of the carapace are placed near the sides.

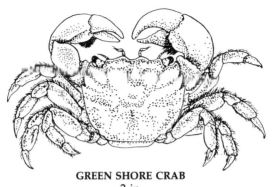

GREEN SHORE CRAB
2 in

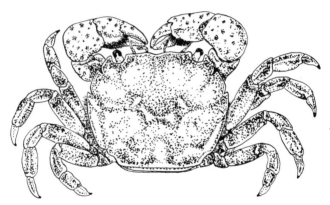

PURPLE SHORE CRAB
2 in

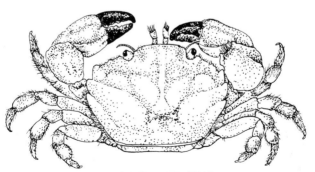

BLACK-CLAWED CRAB
1 in

■RED ROCK CRAB
Cancer productus

A large crab seen crawling in shallow water of sandy, muddy, and gravelly bays; found hidden under seaweed and large rocks in the lower intertidal zone of cobble beaches. Heavy carapace (shell) is brick red; claw tips are black. Front edge of carapace has 6 to 8 large, evenly spaced, dull spines; rear of carapace curves inward along the middle. Carapace is smaller than the Dungeness Crab's but claws are heavier and are so strong that they can crack open snails and barnacles. Grows to about 6 inches.

The **Oregon Rock Crab** (*Cancer oregonensis*) looks like a smaller (under 2 inches), rounder version of the Red Rock Crab. Found intertidally under rocks, but prefers to hide in the empty shells of Giant Barnacles; mostly subtidal locally.

■DUNGENESS CRAB
Cancer magister

Shell (carapace) is grayish brown; legs tan; claw tips are lighter. Front edge of carapace has a row of 10 or so small, sharply pointed spines; rear edges of carapace are straighter than Red Rock Crab's. To 8 inches or more.

Though seen in shallows (especially in Eelgrass beds) the Dungeness Crab is mainly a subtidal species. Gravid (egg-carrying) females have been found in large aggregations at 120-foot depths off Everett's Port Gardner. Females told by broad, U-shaped abdominal flap underneath for carrying eggs; males have narrow, V-shaped flap. Prefers sandy or muddy bottom. Can burrow backwards up to its eyes. Eats small clams. An important commercial species. Collecting is regulated.

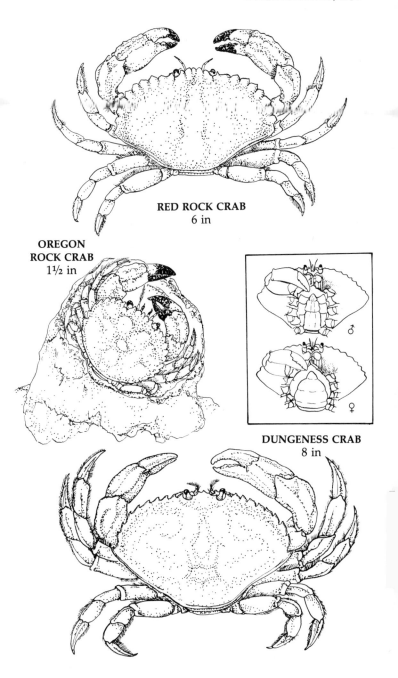

RED ROCK CRAB
6 in

**OREGON
ROCK CRAB**
1½ in

♂

♀

DUNGENESS CRAB
8 in

KELP CRAB
Pugettia producta

Called a "spider" crab because of its slender legs and claws. The greenish brown carapace is shaped like a shield, somewhat longer than wide. Carapace of a large specimen can reach 4 inches from front to back. Found among seaweed on rocky shores; less often in Eelgrass beds; also common subtidally on pilings and bridge supports.

GRACEFUL CRAB
Pugettia gracilis

A close relative of the Kelp Crab but much smaller; its reddish brown carapace rarely grows longer than 1 inch. Its carapace is more rounded and is edged with spines; the two central points ("rostral horns") project far to the front. A "decorator" crab: covers spiny carapace with live algae of many species. When it molts (sheds its exoskeleton in the course of growth), it takes bits of algae from the old carapace to cultivate on the new one. Found intertidally and subtidally in kelp and Eelgrass beds.

DECORATOR CRAB
Oregonia gracilis

Another "spider" crab; legs are relatively long, extremely slender, and sharply pointed. Even more bizarrely decorated than the Graceful Crab. Cements a mix of organisms (seaweeds, sponges, hydroids, bryozoans) over carapace and legs, handling them with delicate pincers and sticking them on with a gluey secretion from its mouth. Beneath this bushy mass, the rough carapace is rounded at the back and pointed at the front, with pronounced rostral horns and a dorsal "tooth" behind eyes. Total length may reach 2 inches.

SHARP-NOSED CRAB
Scyra acutifrons

Another "decorator." Resembles the Decorator Crab, especially when covered with a heavy growth of algae and other organisms. But claws and legs are relatively shorter and stouter; its rostral horns are stouter and more divergent; its carapace is rougher. To 1½ inches. Found among kelp.

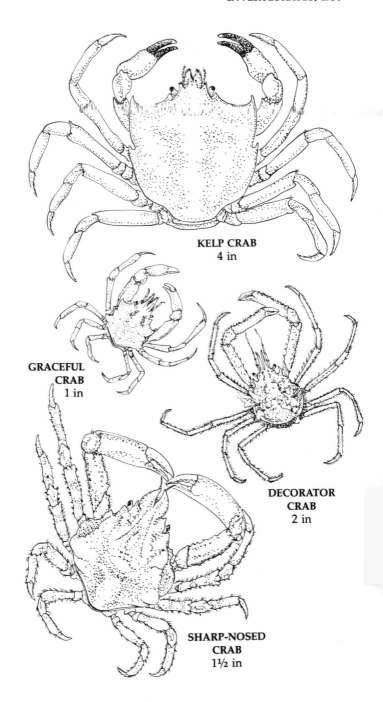

KELP CRAB
4 in

**GRACEFUL
CRAB**
1 in

**DECORATOR
CRAB**
2 in

**SHARP-NOSED
CRAB**
1½ in

◼◼◼Echinoderms

Phylum Echinodermata

Spiny-skinned marine animals; phylum includes sea stars, brittle stars, sea cucumbers, sea urchins, and sand dollars. Mobile spines, tiny pincers (pedicellariae), and muscular tube-feet protrude from calcareous or leathery outer covering. Radially symmetrical in 5 parts; easy to see in 5-rayed sea stars but less obvious (and often less symmetrical) in sea urchins, sea cucumbers, and sand dollars.

◼◼◼Sea Stars

Class Asteroidea

Sea stars (starfishes) are 5- to many-rayed echinoderms; common in the intertidal and subtidal zones. Move along on hundreds of small tube-feet beneath the arms. Tube-feet are muscular but also connected with a hydraulic water-vascular system that controls the amount of suction in the tiny cup at the end. Most sea stars have clusters of small calcareous jaws (pedicellariae) on tiny stalks on upper surface; these jaws nip at small animals or plants that might settle on its surface. Mouth is beneath the central disk. Most feed on barnacles, mussels, and clams; but some feed on other sea stars, and a few are filter-feeders.

◼SUNFLOWER STAR

Pycnopodia helianthoides

Our largest and most spectacular sea star. Arms (rays) are slender but short; usually 20 to 24 (depending on age and recent losses). The large central disk is often humped, though it flattens out when stranded. Usually reddish orange with some purple. Mostly subtidal, but is sometimes stranded during very low tides. Can move rapidly and is a powerful predator. Prefers sea urchins; but many other animals—scallops, abalones, and sea cucumbers—show a dramatic escape response to its presence.

◼SUN STAR

Solaster stimpsoni

Attractive. Orange-red, with bluish gray stripes down center of 10 slender arms. Medium-size disk. Grows to 15 inches.

Rare intertidally but common subtidally. Feeds on small sea cucumbers. Preyed on by the subtidal sun star, *Solaster dawsoni*, which feeds on it exclusively.

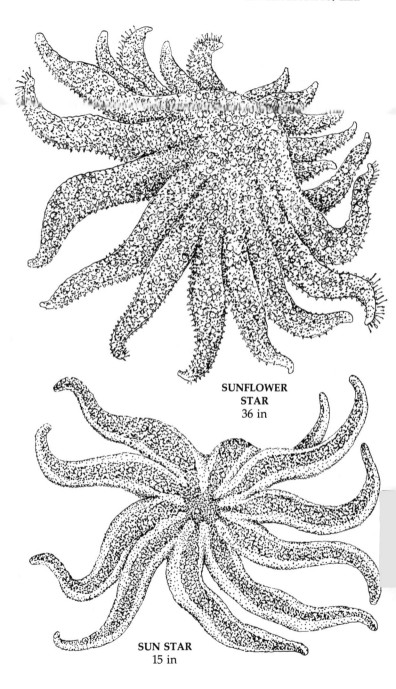

**SUNFLOWER
STAR**
36 in

SUN STAR
15 in

■ PURPLE (Ochre) SEA STAR

Pisaster ochraceus

Five broad rays (arms) are stiff and bumpy, patterned with lines of very short white spines. Purple phase is prevalent locally; ochre phase more common on outer coast. To 12 inches.

Common on rocky beaches and on pilings. At low tide can be found, alone or clumped together, under overhanging rocks, in rocky tide channels, or on pilings. When tide is up, it climbs up to feed on beds of mussels and barnacles, its favorite foods. Also eats limpets and snails. Feeds by humping over prey and forcing shells apart; then inserts its extrudable belly to dissolve and devour the inner parts.

■ MOTTLED SEA STAR

Evasterias troschelii

Our other common intertidal sea star. Five long, slender rays meet almost in the center of the small central disk. Covered with small, whitish spines. Variable color: shades of gray, green, brown, flesh, or red. Grows to about 12 inches across (maximum 20 inches).

In the San Juan and Canadian Gulf islands *Evasterias* might be confused with **Orthasterias koehleri**, which is otherwise mostly subtidal. *Orthasterias* is even more slender than *Evasterias*, with longer spines; its color is often brick red with blotches of bluish gray.

■ BLOOD STAR

Henricia leviuscula

Usually a bright red-orange. The 5 rays are smooth and slender with almost no central disk. Grows to less than 5 inches across. Found on rocky shores among Surfgrass, in tide pools, or at lowest tides. Feeds mostly on sponges.

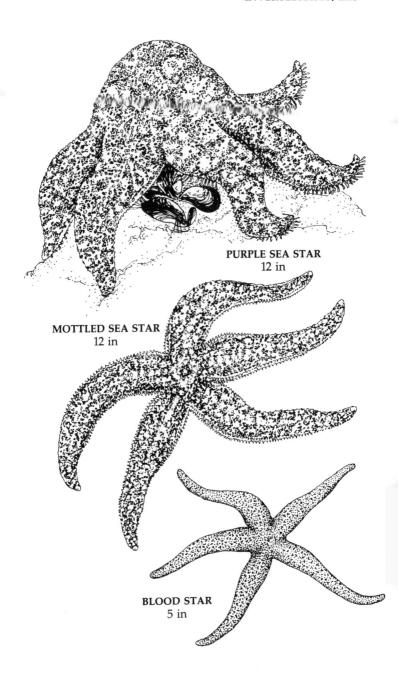

PURPLE SEA STAR
12 in

MOTTLED SEA STAR
12 in

BLOOD STAR
5 in

■ VERMILION SEA STAR
Mediaster aequalis

Narrow, pointed arms meet in a relatively large disk. Large plates border the edges of its 5 rays. Smells like exploded gunpowder. To 6 inches. Mostly subtidal. Found with Sea Pens, on which it feeds. Also eats filamentous diatoms and detritus.

■ SIX-RAYED SEA STAR
Leptasterias hexactis

It is our only 6-rayed sea star (except for very young *Pycnopodia*). Very common but small and inconspicuous. Color variable: tan to greenish gray to black. To less than 4 inches at maturity. Feeds on barnacles, limpets, mussels, and snails.

Our only sea star that broods its young. In winter groups congregate under rocks to spawn. Female humps over her eggs, cleaning and tending them for up to 2 months without eating.

■ Brittle Stars
Class Ophiuroidea

Five slender, flexible rays extend from a distinct central disk. Move by writhing their rays, rather than by "walking" on tube-feet as sea stars do. Lack tiny pincers (pedicellariae). Feed on small detritus.

■ BRITTLE STAR
Amphipholis squamata

Gray above, whitish below. Grows to over 1 inch (including arms). Broods its eggs and young in "bursal" pockets near bases of arms. Common under rocks on muddy sand. Eats diatoms and detritus.

■ RED-AND-TAN BRITTLE STAR
Ophiopholis aculeata

Central disk is fringed with red; center is tan. Colorful spiny arms are red and brown with light line down center. Found in crevices at lower levels of rocky shores of San Juan and Canadian Gulf islands.

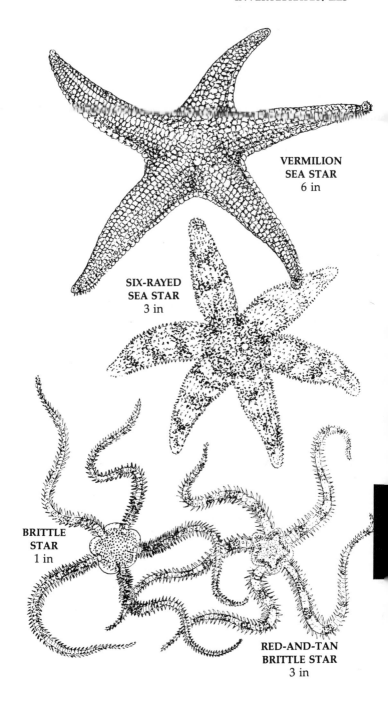

**VERMILION
SEA STAR**
6 in

**SIX-RAYED
SEA STAR**
3 in

**BRITTLE
STAR**
1 in

**RED-AND-TAN
BRITTLE STAR**
3 in

■ Sea Urchins and Sand Dollar   *Class* Echinoidea

Sea urchins have long, mobile spines connected to a hemispheric shell (test). Move on extensible tube-feet that stick out among spines. Feed on detritus and seaweed, which they chew with a 5-plate pinching jaw (Aristotle's lantern) that sits within the mouth hole on the underside of the test. Sea urchin pedicellariae have 3 jaws rather than the sea star's 2. Called "sea eggs" by Indians who collected them for yellow gonads ("yolk").

Sand dollars have flattened tests and tiny spines. Anus is beneath test, rather then on top as in urchins.

■ RED SEA URCHIN   *Strongylocentrotus franciscanus*

Our largest urchin; shell (test) grows to 5 inches. Long, dark, slender spines extend 2 inches from test. Common subtidally; seen in lower tide pools and surge channels on rocky shores. Usually immobile but can move rather rapidly when approached by the Sunflower Star or other predator. Feeds on pieces of drifting kelp, which it captures with its long, mobile spines. (It will gently grab your finger, if placed between the spines.)

■ GREEN SEA URCHIN   *Strongylocentratos droebachiensis*

Shell (test) is a dull, light green. Grows to about 3 inches. Spines are short and crowded. Found in lower level tide pools and surge channels of rocky shores. More mobile than the Red Sea Urchin. It often feeds on pieces of kelp trapped by the spines of the larger species.

The **Purple Sea Urchin** (*Strongylocentrotus purpuratus*) is the same size as Green Sea Urchin (to 3 inches), but spines are longer and less crowded. Found mostly on outer coast in strong wave action; sometimes in San Juan and Canadian Gulf islands in lower level tide pools and surge channels. Digs protective hollows in soft rock; often seen in large clusters.

■ SAND DOLLAR   *Dendraster excentricus*

Sand dollars are in the same class as sea urchins, but shells (tests) are flattened. When alive, the many tiny spines and tube-feet give the animal a reddish, velvety look. When washed up on shore, the grayish test shows echinoderm heritage by an attractive 5-armed pattern of tiny holes. In our species the pattern is always excentric (off center); thus the specific name *excentricus*. Grows to 3 inches. Lives subtidally, often in huge masses, half buried in sand. Feeds on diatoms and detritus, which are moved to the mouth by tiny cilia (moveable hairs).

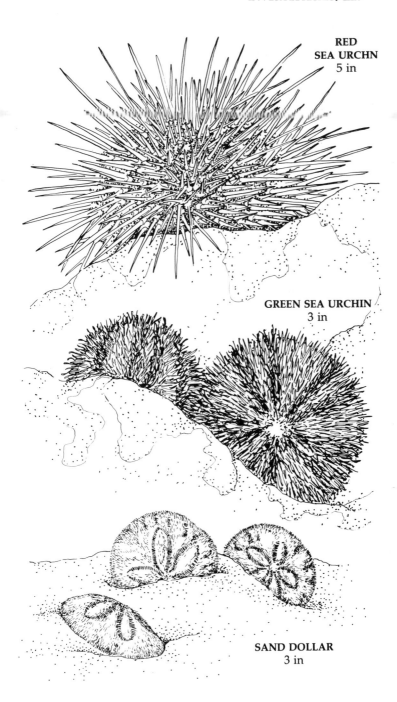

**RED
SEA URCHN**
5 in

GREEN SEA URCHIN
3 in

SAND DOLLAR
3 in

■■■■ **Sea Cucumbers** *Class* Holothuroidea

Sea cucumbers are echinoderms, but much unlike sea stars. The five radial sections are elongated and unequal. Body is soft or leathery; skeletal plates that remain are scattered through body. Feed mainly on detritus.

■**ORANGE CUCUMBER** *Cucumaria miniata*

very common under and between rocks at lower levels of cobble and rocky beaches. When extended, the bright orange or dark maroon tentacles form feathery branches to collect detritus; they retract into the duller maroon body when exposed or threatened. Body is lined with 5 rows of tiny tube-feet.

■**GIANT SEA CUCUMBER** *Parastichopus californicus*

Our largest sea cucumber, averaging 16 inches long. Very common subtidally; often seen in low tide pools or crevices of rocky beaches. Tubular, dark red body is covered with sharp, fleshy spikes. Flabby out of water. Moves on tube-feet in three rows along lower body. Can also rear up and swim with slow undulations when approached by Sunflower Star. Cleans detritus from moplike tentacles surrounding the mouth. Echinoderm heritage is shown by 5 rows of internal muscles, which can be eaten.

■**WHITE SEA CUCUMBER** *Eupentacta quinquesemita*

Cream colored; tinged with orange. Covered with 5 bristly rows of short, slender tube-feet. Bushy oral tentacles bring detritus and plankton to the mouth. To 3½ inches. Lives in crevices between rocks or among mussels or tube worms on flats and pilings. Mostly subtidal.

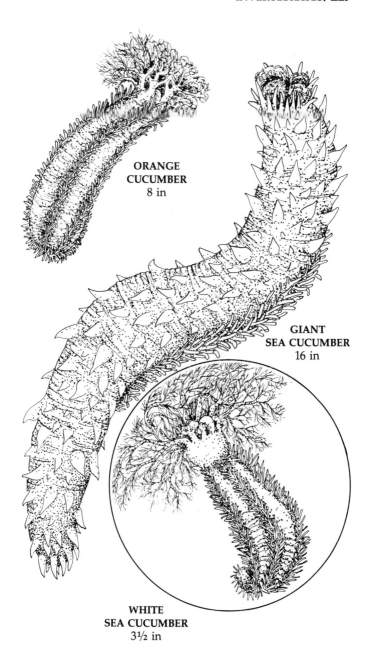

**ORANGE
CUCUMBER**
8 in

**GIANT
SEA CUCUMBER**
16 in

**WHITE
SEA CUCUMBER**
3½ in

■■■■ Urochordates
Phylum Urochordata

■■■ Ascidians
Class Ascidiacea

Simple-looking animals; but actually are quite advanced invertebrates. During early development as small, nonfeeding "tadpoles," they have a notochord (simple spinal chord) and other vetebratelike structures. Later the complex body is reabsorbed, and it reverts to the lifestyle of a sponge. Formerly placed in the Chordate phylum.

Some ascidians are solitary, some colonial. The ones we call "sea squirts" are solitary. Social ascidians like *Aplidium* are embedded in a jellylike matrix; individuals are connected by creeping "stems" (stolons), from which new ones grow. Many local species; the 2 below are the most common.

■ WARTY SEA SQUIRT
Pyura haustor

Solitary, but sometimes grows in pairs or groups. Attaches to rocks at its base. Two red siphons extending from the wrinkled, globular body are used to filter (through a sheet of mucus) plankton from the surrounding water. Brownish red. Grows to a height of about 2 inches.

■ SEA PORK
Aplidium spp.

A common colonial ascidian that forms thick slabs on rocks. The pink, brown, or orange individuals are encased in clear jelly; connected by creeping stolons, from which new individuals grow.

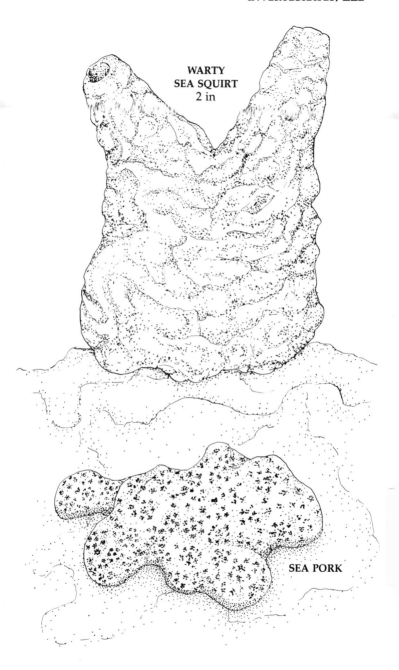

**WARTY
SEA SQUIRT**
2 in

SEA PORK

SEAWEEDS

The 3 major divisions of multi-celled marine algae—Browns, Reds, and Greens—differ mainly in types and ratios of photosynthetic pigments. Being almost weightless in water, they do not need woody structures for support. Because they absorb minerals and carbon dioxide directly from seawater, they do not need a vascular system or true roots. The plant (thallus) consists of leaflike "blade," stemlike "stipe," and rootlike or discoid "holdfast."

Many species have alternate generations (similar in some species, quite dissimilar in others). The sporophyte generation produces spores, gametophyte generation produces male and female gametes.

Some species are adapted to low light conditions, but turbidity caused by plankton blooms and river silt limits most local species to depths less than 100 feet. For every conspicuous species, there are many invisible, single-celled algal species (diatoms, dinoflagellates, etc.), which grow in incredible numbers in the plankton and form the base of the sea's entire web of food and energy. Only a few seaweeds have common names; most naturalists use the generic name in any case.

■■■Brown Algae   *Division* Phaeophyta

Typically brown, yellow-brown, or olive green. Larger species are called "kelp" after the Middle English word for the soap maker's potash derived from burning some species.

■BULL KELP   *Nereocystis luetkeana*

Long (up to about 80 feet), slender, brown stipe; ends in large, hollow float from which spread 2 groups of broad, flat blades (to about 25 feet long, 5 inches wide). Massive rootlike holdfast.

Attaches to rocks just beyond lowest tides. Entire growth takes place from spring to fall (to several inches per day). Most plants die off during first winter; release spores that become the microscopic, overwintering gametophyte generation.

Bull kelp beds shelter schools of fishes; seabirds rest in calmed sea around fronds. Large tangles are washed ashore by winter storms; leathery stalks may last months. Hollow bulbs were used by coastal Indians as water vessels; long stipes were knotted end-to-end as fishing line for Halibut.

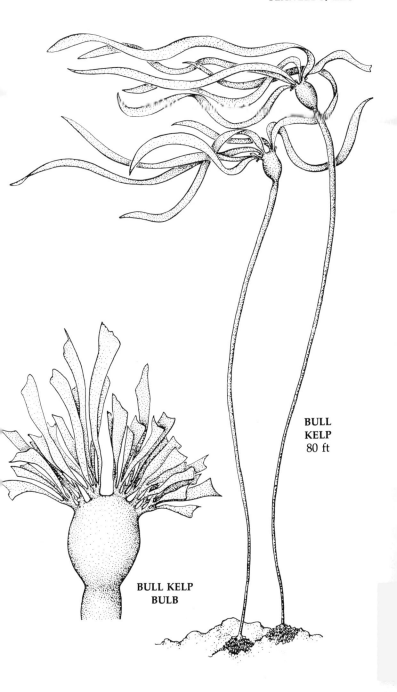

**BULL
KELP**
80 ft

**BULL KELP
BULB**

■ **ALARIA (Wing Kelp)**   *Alaria marginata*
One of our largest kelps. Deep brown to olive. Wavy-edged blade is long, slender, smooth. Cylindrical stipe continues as prominent midrib. Cluster of smaller, oval-shaped blades (sporophylls) grow from stipe; these produce spores from large blisters (sori) that cover most of the sporophyll. Rootlike holdfast is small but stout. Grows to 10 feet long. Blade to 8 inches wide, frequently tattered. Intertidal to shallow subtidal.

■ **LAMINARIA (Sugar Wrack)**   *Laminaria saccharina*
Another distinctive large kelp. Brown blade can reach 10 feet long; width about ¼ of length. Mature plant has 2 rows of raised or lowered patches (bullations) running length of blade; younger plant has less regular pattern of bullations. Rootlike holdfast; short, cylindrical stipe. Found at lowest tide levels or upper subtidal. Called "sugar wrack" because of sweet taste; contains mannitol (a form of sugar).

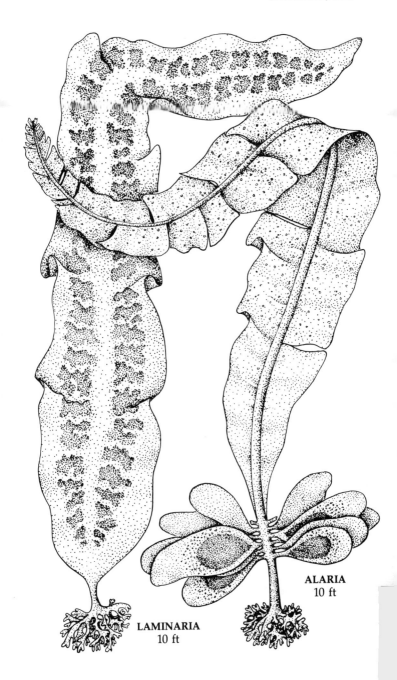

LAMINARIA
10 ft

ALARIA
10 ft

■ **SEA COLANDER** *Agarum fimbriatum*

Blade has perforated, crinkly surface. Prominent, smooth midrib. Margin of wide, brown blade is irregularly toothed giving it a fringed look; end is often frayed. Stipe is short and flattened above with small outgrowths below the blade. Blade grows to 5 feet long, 2 feet wide. Grows on rocks from lowest tide levels to shallow subtidal.

A related species, *Agarum cribrosum*, has wider blade; smoother, wavy margin. To 3 feet long, 2 feet wide. Found in upper subtidal zone, sometimes in thick growths.

■ **SEERSUCKER** *Costaria costata*

Broad, flat blade; rounded at base. Five prominent ribs; 3 raised on one side, 2 on the other. Rows of raised or lowered patches (bullations) between ribs. Dark brown; turns green when dead. Short stipe is cylindrical at base, divides into ribs. Grows to 3 feet or more; blade to 1 foot wide.

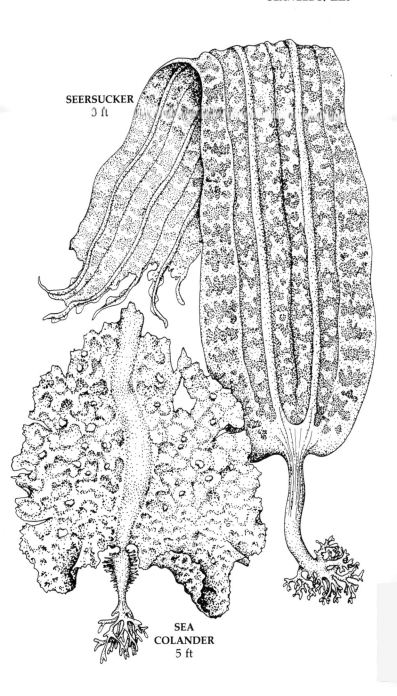

SEERSUCKER
3 ft

SEA COLANDER
5 ft

■ ROCKWEED (Popping Wrack) *Fucus gardneri(distichus)*

Flattened, branching blade has raised midrib. Blade of mature plant ends in warty, swollen tip (receptacle) that produces gametes. Greenish to yellowish brown. Holdfast is thickened button. Covers upper levels of rocky beaches throughout the world's cool seas. Grows to about 12 inches.

The blades of a similar species, *Fucus spiralis*, are twisted, espe-
cially when dry. Found around the San Juan and Canadian Gulf islands and outer coast of Vancouver Island.

■ SEA CABBAGE *Hedophyllum sessile*

Forms loose clump of broad, brown blades; may be blistered or smooth; covered with large mucilage ducts. As plant matures, the short stipe disappears. A broad, rootlike holdfast holds the blades to the rock. Blades sometimes wrap around themselves like a loose head of cabbage; often split by wave action. To 24 inches long, about half as wide; plants larger on outer coast. Spore-producing bodies (sori) are present near base of blades. Abundant on rocky shores from midtide levels to upper subtidal.

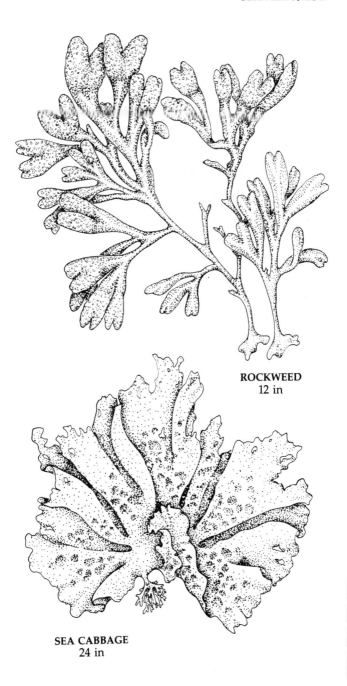

ROCKWEED
12 in

SEA CABBAGE
24 in

■**FEATHER BOA** *Egregia menziesii*
Very long, flattened midrib covered with tiny bumps. Branches repeatedly. Many small slender blades (2 inches long) grow from edges of midrib; most are flattened but some are swollen to form oblong floats. Young specimen has wide blades and no floats. Blades are brown to olive; stipe is darker. Rootlike holdfast. Grows to 15 feet. Found on rocky coast. Subtidal to lower intertidal.

■**SARGASSUM** *Sargassum muticum*
Small, flattened leaflets, club-shaped reproductive structures, and tiny floats grow from thin, branched stalks. Stalks arise from thick stipe that ends in thin, flattened branches. Discoid holdfast. Yellowish brown. Reaches length of 3 to 4 feet or more in protected bays. Often floats loose and drifts ashore. Introduced from Japan.

Another local species in the sargassum family, **Chain Bladder** (*Cystoseira geminata*), is similar but floats are in chains (the final one pointed, not round as in *Sargassum*). Grows to 10 feet or more.

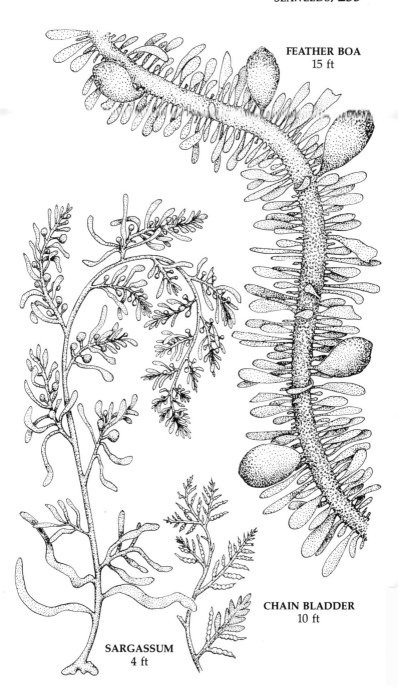

FEATHER BOA
15 ft

CHAIN BLADDER
10 ft

SARGASSUM
4 ft

■WIDE DESMARESTIA
Desmarestia ligulata

Wide, flattened central axis; narrower, secondary branches are opposite; very small tertiary leaflets; all in same plane. Shape variable.
Young specimen has fewer but wider branches. Discoid holdfast.
Short, cylindrical stipe flattens to become main axis. Dark to yellowish brown. Grows to 2 feet or more (maximum 8 feet). Found at
lowest intertidal and upper subtidal zones

Note: Cell sap contains sulfuric acid; will dissolve other seaweeds if collected in same container.

■THIN DESMARESTIA
Desmarestia viridis

Narrow, cylindrical main stalk; many finer opposite branches; hairlike tertiary branches. Small discoid holdfast. Cylindrical stipe; thick
at base but gradually narrows as it branches. Dark brown. Grows to 2
feet.

Note: Cell sap contains sulfuric acid; will dissolve other seaweeds if collected in same container.

■SCYTOSIPHON (Whip Tube)
Scytosiphon lomentaria

Slender, flabby tubular blades; often spiral and sometimes pinched
into sausage-shaped segments. Light olive to dark brown. Length to
20 inches. Width around ⅓ inch or less. Found on rocky coast; sometimes at edges of shallow pools. Prefers lower tide levels.

■LEATHESIA
Leathesia difformis

Small, convoluted, globular sac. Yellow-brown to olive. Spongy tex-
ture; breaks into mass of filaments when squeezed. Diameter up to 4
inches. Found on rocky beaches in and around tide pools attached to
rocks or to other seaweeds.

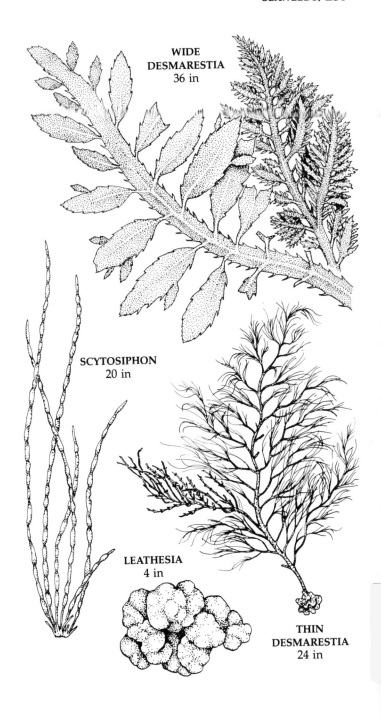

WIDE DESMARESTIA
36 in

SCYTOSIPHON
20 in

LEATHESIA
4 in

THIN DESMARESTIA
24 in

■ Red Algae   *Division* Rhodophyta

Vary from pink to brown to purple to blackish red. Most are small and delicate. Coralline species are hardened by calcium carbonate; some form thin crusts on rocks.

■ IRIDESCENT SEAWEED   *Iridea (Iridaea) cordata*

Broad, slick, rubbery blades; margins sometimes ruffled. Bluish iridescence in water; deep purple-red when dry. Young plant is particularly bright blue. Grows to 3 feet. Plant is perennial but dies back to holdfast in winter. A good source of carrageenan, a thickening agent.

■ TURKISH TOWEL   *Gigartina exasperata*

Broad, thick blades covered with hundreds of tall, stiff outgrowths (papillae). Brick to purplish red; somewhat iridescent when wet. Discoid holdfast sometimes gives rise to multiple blades. Plant is perennial but dies back to just the holdfast in winter. Grows to 18 inches long; 5 to 10 inches wide. Found in lower intertidal zone of rocky or cobbly beaches; also grows subtidally to 60-foot depth. A good source of carrageenan, a thickening agent.

■ MASTOCARPUS (Gigartina)   *Mastocarpus papillatus*

Thin, leathery blades covered with small, varied-size warts (papillae). Blades are often split. Dark, brownish red. Grows to 6 inches. Found at midtide levels or below.

Mastocarpus produces male and female gametes that produce a "Petrocelis" stage, which is so dissimilar that it was once considered a separate species in a different genus. Purplish black lumps look like tar spots. Remains for many years in Petrocelis stage, producing spores that become in turn the flat, red, warty Mastocarpus stage.

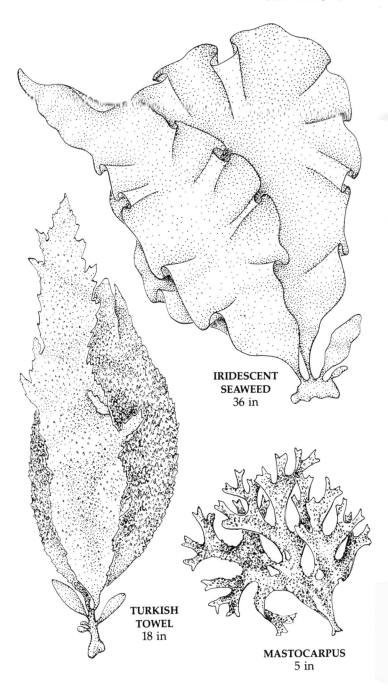

**IRIDESCENT
SEAWEED**
36 in

**TURKISH
TOWEL**
18 in

MASTOCARPUS
5 in

■ HALOSACCION   *Halosaccion glandiforme*

Erect, sausage-shaped sacs. Yellow-brown to olive green to reddish purple. Attaches by discoid holdfast. When exposed, the sacs stay partially filled with water. Commonly grows to 5 inches. Found at midtide levels, often massed together.

■ CUP AND SAUCER   *Constantinea simplex*

Circular, purplish red blade on a tough, cylindrical stalk; resembles terrestrial cup fungus. Stipe grows up through frayed "saucer" of previous blade; grows "cup" of new blade. Scars remain on stalk where old blades have worn away. Stalk grows to 4 inches; blades to 4 inches in diameter. Found just below low tide.

■ PORPHYRA   *Porphyra perforata* and *Porphyra torta*

Thin brownish purple blade; turns black and rubbery when exposed; brittle when dry. Blade is perforated; ruffled near edges; iridescent. Attaches to rocks by a tiny discoid holdfast. Grows to 2 feet long. Cultivated as a condiment worldwide (called "laver" by Europeans, "nori" by Japanese). Two similar species: *Porphyra perforata* dominates in spring and summer; *Porphyra torta* in winter.

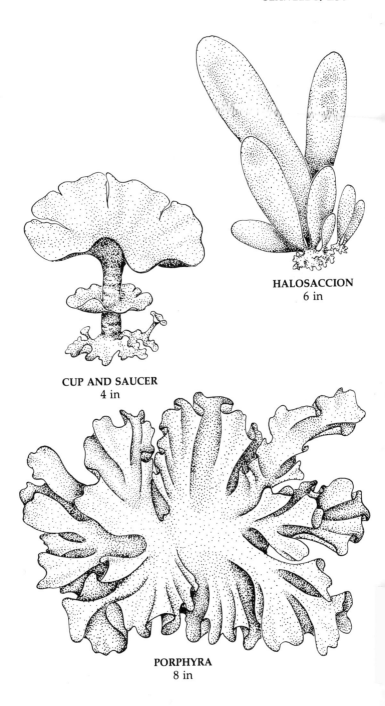

HALOSACCION
6 in

CUP AND SAUCER
4 in

PORPHYRA
8 in

■ DULSE
Palmaria mollis

Thin blades; irregularly divided; wavy edges. Brownish to reddish purple. Blades 5 to 20 inches long, by 1 to 6 inches wide. Short stipe. Many blades arise from a single discoid holdfast. Found at upper tide levels. High in vitamin C. Eaten as a condiment worldwide.

■ ENDOCLADIA
Endocladia muricata

Forms tough but delicate-looking tufts, 1 to 3 inches tall; becomes wirelike when dry. Dark red, brown, or black. Many thalli arise from each discoid holdfast. When examined closely, cylindrical branches seen studded with short, spined tubercles. Found with Acorn Barnacles at highest tide levels; forms a miniature forest for tiny animals.

■ BLACK PINE
Neorhodomela (Rhodomela) larix

Tufts of small, thin, needlelike branchlets spiral around cylindrical stipe. Dark, blackish brown. Clusters of branches arise from short stipe. Discoid holdfast. Commonly to 4 inches long but can reach 1 foot. Found at midtide levels and in tide pools higher up.

The somewhat similar *Odonthalia floccosa* branches more but the slender leaflets are not clustered.

■ VEINED FAN
Hymenena flabelligera

Resembles a fan. Flat, ruffly blade branches 2 to 4 times before ending in rounded tips. Lower portion of blade has distinct midrib, which branches into thin, dark lines. Single, broad discoid holdfast gives rise to many thalli; some prostrate, some erect. Pink to brownish purple. Grows to 12 inches. Found at lowest tide levels.

Two similar species are found locally. *Botryoglossum farlowianum* is edged with crinkly, small ruffles and lacks veins. *Cryptopleura lobulifera* has wavy ruffles; also lacks veins.

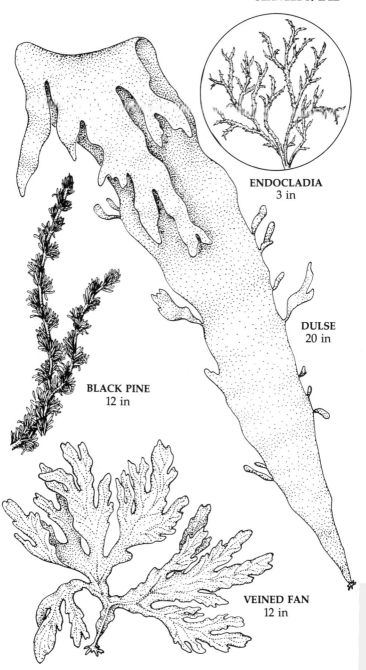

ENDOCLADIA
3 in

DULSE
20 in

BLACK PINE
12 in

VEINED FAN
12 in

■ Coralline Red Algae

A group of red algae that deposits limey salts around segments of the thallus. In the upright species the joints between these segments are not calcified, and so the plant can sway. Encrusting species cover surfaces of rock or shell.

■ BEAD CORALS   *Calliarthron* spp. and *Bossiella* spp.

Pinkish; white at tips. Similar to the Erect Coralline (below), but segments are shorter; reproductive organs form bumps on segments rather than swellings at tips. *Bossiella's* segments are flattened; branching is irregular; 1 to 6 inches tall. *Calliarthron's* segments are sometimes flattened, sometimes cylindrical, but never swollen at tips. Branching is opposite; 3 to 6 inches tall. Found from midlevel tide pools to upper subtidal.

■ ERECT CORALLINE   *Corallina vancouveriensis*

Forms erect, feathery thalli 2 to 4 inches tall that arise from encrusting layer. Bright pink to purple, often whitish at tips; whole plant turns white when dead. Each cell is covered by hard calcium carbonate, softer at joints. Branching is opposite. Lower segments are somewhat flattened; longer than wide. Upper segments cylindrical; some are swollen at tips (reproductive structures). Found from midlevel tide pools to upper subtidal.

■ PINK ROCK CRUSTS   *Lithothamnion* complex

A group of similar species of coralline algae. Form thin, bright pink, lichenlike crusts on rocks and shells; sometimes the crusts overlap and build up. Very common at lowest tide levels and upper subtidal. Spores shed from pores in white dots on surface. Along with the layer of tiny algae that colonize it, pink rock crusts are grazed on by Lined Chiton and by Whitecap Limpet (on which it often grows).

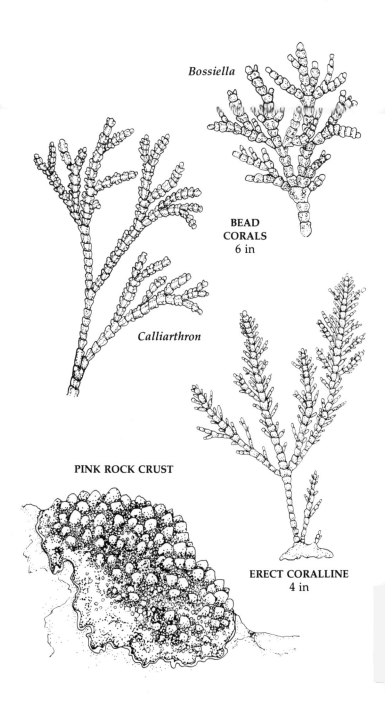

Bossiella

BEAD CORALS
6 in

Calliarthron

PINK ROCK CRUST

ERECT CORALLINE
4 in

▄▄ Green Algae   *Division* Chlorophyta

Vary from grass green to olive to blackish green. Many species form wide, translucent sheets or long, narrow tubes.

■ ENTEROMORPHA   *Enteromorpha linza*

Closely related to Sea Lettuce, but forms long, thin, yellowish green blades. Blades are tubular at the base but flattened above; often wrinkled at margins. Attaches to rocks, pilings, or other algae by tiny holdfast. Often the dominant species in estuaries. Grows larger on mud flats (up to 16 inches) than on pilings.

The smaller *Enteromorpha intestinalis* forms thin, yellowish green tubes, which grow to 10 inches or more. Often found in great masses near rivers or where fresh water seeps down cliffs.

■ SEA LETTUCE   *Ulva fenestrata (lactuca)*

Forms thin, bright green sheets; 2 cells thick. Crinkly when dry. Tubelike when young. One form (formerly *Ulva lactuca*) flattens into broad blades, sometimes ruffled or split; to 6 inches long. The other form develops longer, narrow blades, many holes and tears in surface. Both are abundant on floats. Attaches to rocks by irregular holdfast; at upper tide levels. Sometimes floats freely over shallow, muddy bays.

■ ULVALIKE   *Monostroma-Ulvaria-Kornmannia-Blidingia* complex
SPECIES

Formerly lumped together as *Monostroma*. All grow as broad, flat blades resembling Sea Lettuce, but are only one cell thick. Young specimen is hollow sac; later opens into thin sheet. *Ulvaria* is the largest (to 10 inches). The smaller *Kornmannia* (to 2 inches) grows on Eelgrass and Surfgrass. *Blidingia* genus has several species; all have many thin blades growing from cushionlike holdfast. All attach to floats and intertidal rocks by small, irregular holdfasts; also float freely in shallow water.

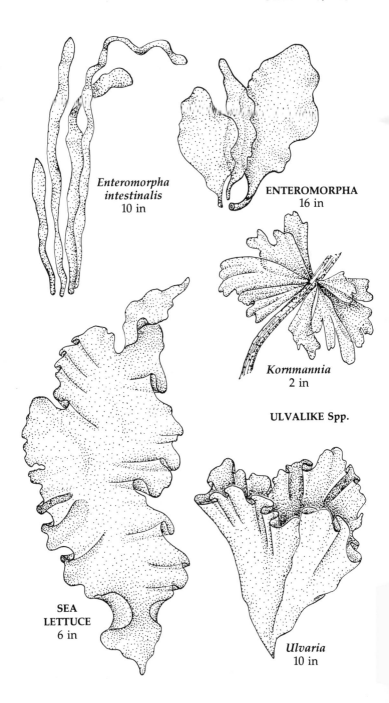

Enteromorpha intestinalis
10 in

ENTEROMORPHA
16 in

Kormannia
2 in

ULVALIKE Spp.

SEA LETTUCE
6 in

Ulvaria
10 in

■ACROSIPHONIA
Acrosiphonia (Spongomorpha) coalita

Bright green branches often hook together to form ropelike complex. Grows to 10 inches. Young specimen forms loose tufts; later develops into long, branched filaments from strings of single cells. Holdfast is a small mass of tiny rootlets. Attaches to rocks or other algae at mid- to lower tide levels. Sexual generation forms cysts in blade of red algae species.

■CLADOPHORA
Cladophora columbiana

Forms bright green, mossy clumps 1 to 4 inches tall. Sometimes called "green ball" because young specimen is hemispherical; spreads out when older. Found in crevices at upper tide levels; also on rocks, pilings, and bulkheads. Eight other species of *Cladophora* are found in Pacific Northwest waters; most of the others are finer in texture and form long, tangled strands.

■SEA STAGHORN
Codium fragile

Solid, cylindrical branches are pencil thick, blunt tipped; fork dichotomously. Older specimen droops. Surface is velvety and spongelike. Blackish green but sometimes covered with white fleece. Composed of woven filaments. Holdfast is a broad cushion up to 2 inches wide. Grows 4 to 16 inches tall. Found from midtide levels to upper subtidal. Eaten by *Elysia hedgpethi,* a sacoglossan nudibranch (sea slug with specialized "tooth" for piercing cell wall).

The related *Codium setchellii* is the same color and texture as sea staghorn but forms a simple, spongy crust about half an inch thick. Found at lower tide levels and upper subtidal.

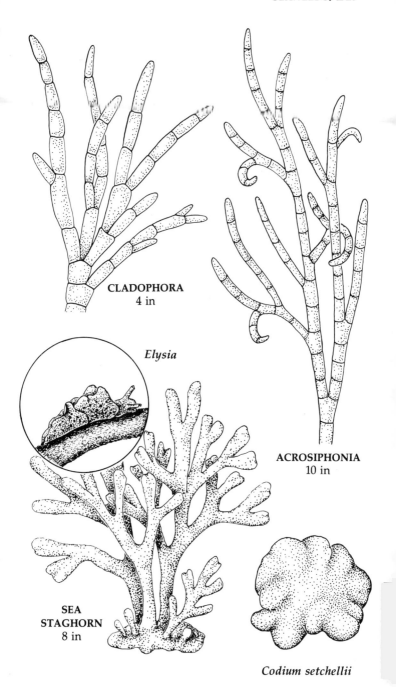

CLADOPHORA
4 in

Elysia

ACROSIPHONIA
10 in

SEA STAGHORN
8 in

Codium setchellii

■ Seagrasses
Family Zosteraceae

A few species of flowering seed plants have adapted to marine life. The 2 below are by far the most conspicuous. Related to freshwater pondweeds.

■ EELGRASS
Zostera marina

Dull green. Thin, strap-shaped leaves to 1/6 inch wide and over 3 feet long. A larger variety (10 to 13 feet long) grows in deep water. Leaves arise from spreading underground stem (rhizome). Inconspicuous flowers are located in curled tips of leaves.

Forms thick beds in muddy areas; from just below tide level to depths of 20 feet. Rhizomes and tangled roots bind mud to create stable habitat. Leaves offer attachment surface for a wide variety of organisms; create shelter for fish and crabs. In summer blades are covered by film of diatoms, bacteria, and detritus. Filmy layer provides food for protozoans, microscopic worms, and small crustaceans; these in turn are eaten by larger turbellarians, nemerteans, hydroids, and jellyfishes. Eelgrass colonies tend to build up in spring and summer, regress in winter.

Zostera japonica is an introduced dwarf species. Blades are only 6 inches long and under 1/8 inch wide. Found locally, mostly in northern area. Grows at uppermost tide levels, above *Zostera marina*.

■ SURFGRASS
Phyllospadix scouleri

Surfgrass (unlike Eelgrass) grows in rocky, wave-swept areas. Long, narrow leaves (to 3 feet long, less than 1/2 inch wide) are bright emerald green; usually bunch together. Leaves arise from fuzzy, creeping stem (stolon) which creeps along the rocks, sending rootlets into tiny crevices. Produces small flowers in tight clusters; pollination takes place underwater.

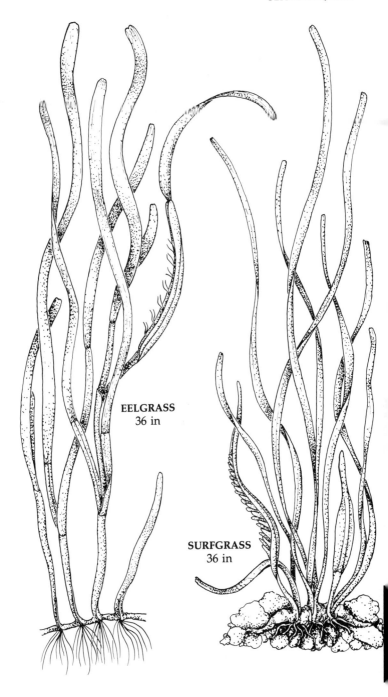

EELGRASS
36 in

SURFGRASS
36 in

Bibliography

MARINE MAMMALS

Angell, T., and K. Balcomb. 1982. *Marine Birds and Mammals of Puget Sound*. Seattle: Washington Sea Grant Publications.

Bigg, M. A., G. Ellis, J. Ford, and K. Balcomb. 1987. *Killer Whales: A Study of Their Identification, Genealogy, and Natural History in British Columbia and Washington State*. Nanaimo, B.C.: Phantom Press & Publications.

Haley, D. ed. 1987. *Marine Mammals of Eastern North Pacific and Arctic Waters*. 2d ed. rev. and enl. Seattle: Pacific Search Press.

McConnaughey, B. H., and E. McConnaughey. 1984. *Pacific Coast*. The Audubon Society Nature Guides. New York: Chanticleer/ Alfred A. Knopf.

Osborne, R. W., J. Calambokidis, and E. Dorsey. 1988. *Marine Mammals of Greater Puget Sound: A Naturalist's Field Guide*. Anacortes, WA: Island Publications.

BIRDS

American Ornithologists' Union. 1983. *Check-list of North American Birds*. 6th ed. (July 1985. Supplement). Lawrence, KA: American Ornithologists' Union.

Angell, T., and K. Balcomb. 1982. *Marine Birds and Mammals of Puget Sound*. Seattle: Washington Sea Grant Publications.

Haley, D. ed. 1984. *Seabirds of Eastern North Pacific and Arctic Waters*. Seattle: Pacific Search Press.

Lewis, M., and F. Sharpe. 1987. *Birds of the San Juan Islands*. Seattle: The Mountaineers Press.

National Geographic Society. 1987. *Field Guide to the Birds of North America*. Washington, D.C.: National Geographic Society.

Robbins, C. S., B. Bruun, H. S. Zim, and A. Singer. 1983. *Birds of North America*. New York: Golden Press.

Udvardy, M. D. F. 1977. *The Audubon Society Field Guide to North American Birds: Western Region*. New York: Alfred A. Knopf.

■ FISHES

American Fisheries Society. 1980. *A List of Common and Scientific Names of Fishes from the United States and Canada*. Spec. Pub., No. 11. Bethesda, MD: American Fisheries Society.

Eschmeyer, W. N., E. Herald, and H. Hammann. 1983. *A Field Guide to the Pacific Coast Fishes*. Boston: Houghton Mifflin Co.

Garrison, K. J., and B. Miller. 1982. *A Review of the Early Life Histories of Puget Sound Fishes*. Seattle: University of Washington Fisheries Research Institute.

Gotshall, D. W. 1981. *Pacific Coast Inshore Fishes*. Los Osos, CA: Sea Challengers.

Hart, J. L. 1973. *Pacific Fishes of Canada*. Fisheries Research Board of Canada, Bull. 180. Ottawa: Dept. of Fisheries and Oceans.

Haw, F., and R. M. Buckley. 1973. *Saltwater Fishing in Washington*. Seattle: Stan Jones Publishing.

Lamb, A., and P. Edgell. 1986. *Coastal Fishes of the Pacific Northwest*. Madiera, B.C.: Harbour Publishing.

Miller, B. S., and S. F. Borton. 1980. *Geographical Distribution of Puget Sound Fishes*. 3 vols. Seattle: University of Washington Fisheries Research Institute/Washington Sea Grant Publications.

Miller, B. S., *et al*. 1978. "Baseline Study Program North Puget Sound, App. D, Nearshore Fishes." Olympia, WA: Washington State Department of Ecology.

Somerton, D., and C. Murray. 1976. *Field Guide to the Fish of Puget Sound and the Northwest Coast*. Seattle: Washington Sea Grant Publications.

Stewart, H. 1977. *Indian Fishing: Early Methods on the Northwest Coast*. Vancouver, B.C.: Douglas & McIntyre.

■ INVERTEBRATES

Abbott, R. T. 1968. *Seashells of North America*. New York: Golden Press.

Kozloff, E. N. 1983. *Seashore Life of the Northern Pacific Coast*. Seattle: University of Washington Press.

————. 1987. *Marine Invertebrates of the Pacific Northwest*. Seattle: University of Washington Press.

McLachlin, D. H., and J. Ayres. 1979. *Sea Creatures*. Happy Camp, CA: Naturegraph Publishers.

McConnaughey, B. H., and E. McConnaughey. 1984. *Pacific Coast*. The Audubon Society Nature Guides. New York: Chanticleer/ Alfred A. Knopf.

Ricketts, E., J. Calvin, and J. W. Hedgpeth. 1968. *Between Pacific Tides*. Palo Alto, CA: Stanford University Press.

Snively, G. 1978. *Exploring the Seashore in British Columbia, Washington and Oregon*. Vancouver, B.C.: Gordon Soules Book Publishers.

■ SEAWEEDS

Guberlet, M. L. 1956. *Seaweeds at Ebb Tide*. Seattle: University of Washington Press.

Kozloff, E. N. 1983. *Seashore Life of the Northern Pacific Coast*. Seattle: University of Washington Press.

Scagel, R. F. 1971. *Guide to Common Seaweeds of British Columbia*. Handbook No. 27. Victoria, B.C.: British Columbia Provincial Museum.

Scagel, R.F., D. Garbary, L. Golden, and M. Hawkes. 1986. "A Synopsis of the Benthic Marine Algae of British Columbia, Northern Washington, and Southeast Alaska." *Phycological Contribution No. 1.* Vancouver, B.C.: University of British Columbia.

Waaland, J. R. 1977. *Common Seaweeds of the Pacific Coast*. Seattle: Pacific Search Press.

Index

256/INDEX

■SEAWEEDS

■ **SEAWEEDS**
(Continued)

Steve Yates is an amateur naturalist and professional free-lance writer, whose articles appear regularly in *Audubon, Smithsonian,* and other national magazines. He lives in Seattle and is currently writing two books on natural history subjects.

The Glo

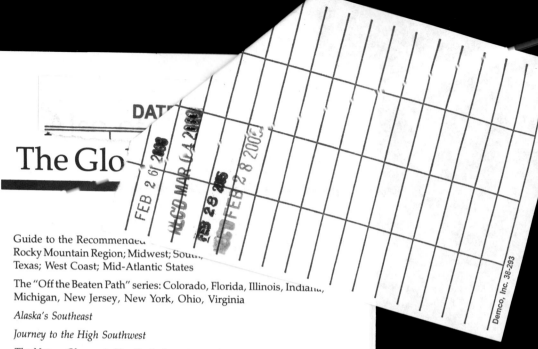

Guide to the Recommended...
Rocky Mountain Region; Midwest; South...
Texas; West Coast; Mid-Atlantic States

The "Off the Beaten Path" series: Colorado, Florida, Illinois, Indiana, Michigan, New Jersey, New York, Ohio, Virginia

Alaska's Southeast

Journey to the High Southwest

The Nature Observer's Handbook, Learning to Appreciate Our Natural World

River Reflections

Melancholy Bay, An Odyssey

Wildflower Folklore

The Wildflower Meadow Book

Garden Flower Folklore

Guide to the National Park Areas, Western States

Guide to the National Park Areas, Eastern States

Parks of the Pacific Coast

Rocky Mountain National Park Hiking Trails

Walks in the Catskills

Walks in the Great Smokies

Cadogan Guides to *Australia, The Caribbean, Greek Islands, Ireland, India, Italian Islands, Scotland, The South of France, Spain,* and *Turkey*

Guide to Western Canada

Guide to Eastern Canada

Bed & Breakfast in California

Bed & Breakfast in the Caribbean

How to Open and Operate a Bed & Breakfast Home

Available at your bookstore or direct from the publisher. For a free catalogue or to place an order, call 1-800-243-0495 (in Connecticut, call 1-800-962-0973) or write to The Globe Pequot Press, 138 West Main Street, Chester, Connecticut 06412.